IMMIGRATION and ETHNICITY in NEW JERSEY HISTORY

by DOUGLAS V. SHAW

D0869369

TRENTON

NEW JERSEY HISTORICAL COMMISSION, DEPARTMENT OF STATE

New Jersey Historical Commission, Department of State
CN 305
Trenton, NJ 08625

Designed by Nancy H. Dallaire and Lee R. Parks
Cover designed by Nancy H. Dallaire

Library of Congress Cataloging-in-Publication Data

Shaw, Douglas V.
    Immigration and ethnicity in New Jersey history/by Douglas V. Shaw.
        p.   cm.—(New Jersey history series; 4)
    Includes bibliographical references.
    ISBN 0-89743-080-8
    1. Immigrants—New Jersey—History. 2. New Jersey—Emigration and immigration—History. 3. Ethnicity—New Jersey—History. I. Title. II. Series.
    JV7037.S53 1994
    304.8'749—dc20
                                           94-21420
                                              CIP

TABLE OF CONTENTS

List of Tables

To my mother and the memory of my father, New Jersey residents for almost forty years.

INTRODUCTION

In New York harbor, closer to the New Jersey shore than to any part of New York, stand two islands important in the story of immigration. One is Liberty Island, from which the Statue of Liberty, the symbol of American freedom, greeted each immigrant ship as it sailed into New York harbor. The other is Ellis Island, for half a century the reception and processing center for millions of European immigrants to America. Today both are national monuments, open to the public, reminding us of the important role that immigration has played in American history.

The poet Walt Whitman called America a nation of nations. Except for Native Americans, all Americans can trace their ancestry to some other place outside the United States. We are all immigrants or the descendants of immigrants. We trace our roots to Europe, Africa, Latin America, and Asia. For some the immigration experience took place generations ago, perhaps as early as 1620, when the *Mayflower* landed at Plymouth Rock. For others it is an event within living memory because our parents, our grandparents, or we ourselves are immigrants, recent arrivals in a process that has yet to end.

The Concept of Ethnicity

Immigrants usually arrive without many physical possessions, but each brings a language, a religion, a set of values, and a moral code, all formed in the country or culture of birth. These are the attributes which make one group of immigrants different from other groups and which form the basis of our concept of ethnicity. One expert has defined ethnicity as membership in "a social group that consciously shares some aspects of a com-

7

mon culture and is defined primarily by descent."[1] It is not a precise term. It overlaps such concepts as "race," which implies a set of common physical attributes, and "nation," which indicates shared political loyalties. An ethnic group is usually assumed to be a minority group in a larger population.

As commonly used in the United States, the term "ethnic groups" names those immigrants (and their descendants) who entered the country after its institutions and culture had been shaped by the original white settlers. It was the English migration and rule of the colonial period (1607–1776) which fixed upon the nation the English language, a democratic form of government, and a set of largely Protestant beliefs and practices. It was this culture to which others arriving later had to adapt.

Immigrants who differed in major ways, such as in language or religion, had to adjust to the demands of their new environment and at the same time find ways to preserve what they could of the values and expectations they carried within themselves. People did not arrive with the intent of being immediately transformed into "Americans." They came to be Irish, Italian, or Hungarian *in* America, to be what they had always been, but in a new place. Hence Catholics and Jews erected churches and synagogues, schools, hospitals, and orphanages. Germans, Italians, and Hispanics have worked to perpetuate their languages beyond the generation of the immigrants themselves. Areas of cities have been associated with particular groups, sometimes for generations, as people have chosen to settle and live out their lives near other people like themselves. What keeps ethnicity alive in the United States is that shared sense of being part of a continuing subgroup within American society.

Leaving Home

Immigration to the United States from Europe began on a large scale after 1830. There were several reasons why people chose to leave one place and resettle in another. First, population growth in Europe made it difficult for some societies to feed and employ all of their members. Second, in the years after 1830 some areas of Europe, notably Ireland and parts of Germany, experienced devastating crop failures. Third, Europe's own political and religious conflicts made emigration to less oppressive environments attractive to many people. Of those who left Europe, slightly more than half came to the United States. The rest chose to settle primarily in Canada, South America, South Africa, or Australia. Immigration to the United States, then, was part of a larger European population movement.

Arriving in the United States

The United States was an attractive destination. In addition to a high degree of political and religious freedom, it offered a variety of economic opportunities. The major period of emigration from Europe began at the same time that industrialization was beginning in the United States. Europeans thus entered an expanding economy that was eager for additional labor.

Further, by arriving in such large numbers, immigrants speeded up the process of industrialization itself. This, in turn, quickened the pace of city growth, or urbanization. More than half the residents of many cities were foreign-born, and in 1880 between 80 percent and 90 percent of the residents of New York and Chicago were foreign-born or the children of immigrants. The transformation of the United States from an underdeveloped agricultural country to an industrial power would have proceeded much more slowly without the continual addition of new workers throughout the nineteenth and early twentieth centuries.

Historical Eras

Historians divide the immigration experience into three periods. From 1830 to 1880 immigration came almost entirely from Ireland, Germany, and Great Britain. This is called the "old" immigration. After 1880 more and more people came from southern and eastern Europe, from Poland, Italy, Hungary, Greece, and elsewhere. This is called the "new" immigration, and it lasted until 1925 when Congress for the first time sharply restricted entry into the United States. Since 1960 immigration has again increased. But this time the major sources are Latin America and Asia rather than Europe. Once again the reasons are oppression and lack of economic opportunity, and once again most arrivals have settled in or near cities.

Effect on New Jersey

New Jersey quickly became home to a large number of immigrants. In every census since 1840 it has been one of the states with the highest proportion of residents born outside the country. The primary reason lies just across the Hudson River. For 150 years New York City has been the nation's most important immigrant port of entry. What has happened in New York City, and to a lesser extent in Philadelphia, has always had a major impact on New Jersey's population and economic development.

As in the nation generally, immigration greatly increased New Jersey's rate of urbanization and industrialization. While some immigrants from every group scattered around the state, most crowded into the three northeastern counties of Essex, Hudson, and Passaic, and especially into the industrial cities of Newark, Jersey City, and Paterson. In 1850 57 percent of New Jersey's immigrants lived in these three counties. Seventy years later, in 1920, the figure was 58 percent. At the same time, fewer than 2 percent lived in the northwestern counties of Sussex, Warren, and Hunterdon.

The distribution of immigrants remains much the same today. In 1980 New Jersey contained 256,000 immigrants who had arrived in the United States between 1970 and 1980. A majority, 51 percent, lived in Essex, Hudson, and Passaic counties. Fewer than one percent lived in Sussex, Warren, and Hunterdon.

Immigration, urbanization, and industrialization created two very different New Jerseys. One was a region of busy factories, screeching freight trains, and densely packed cities with large and growing immigrant populations. The other was a rural and small-town world that remained close to the land and was populated principally by native-born Protestants who traced their roots to colonial settlers.

Ethnic Conflict

When groups of people from different cultures rub shoulders, there is often tension and conflict. People disagree about basic patterns of behavior and about how communities should be organized. In New Jersey, natives and immigrants clashed over such issues as the use and availability of liquor, the role of Catholics and the Catholic church in education and public affairs, and the distribution of political power. A major portion of the story of immigration and ethnicity is the manner in which conflicts arose, were pursued, and finally in some fashion resolved.

Few states have been so continuously shaped and reshaped by immgration as New Jersey. In the colonial period, only Pennsylvania had a more ethnically diverse population. From 1840 to 1920 successive waves of European immigrants helped forge an urban industrial society in what had been a rural farming state.

Since 1960 a third great immigration has again begun to reshape the state. Only five states today hold more recent immigrants than New Jersey. As the state resumes its earlier role as a home to people of other nations and cultures, a review of the history of immigration and ethnicity can help us keep the problems and tensions of the present in better perspective. This pamphlet attempts to make sense of these two related aspects of New Jersey's tangled population history. And important aspects they are, for they are still in the making.

CHAPTER ONE

Creating a Native Stock, 1609–1840

New Netherlands and New Sweden

In 1609 Henry Hudson sailed the *Half Moon* into New York harbor. This began the brief but important history of New Netherland, the first attempt by Europeans to settle in the area that became New Jersey. Permanent Dutch colonists, however, did not arrive until 1626, and then they tended to focus on Manhattan Island and the Hudson River Valley. Between 1630 and 1655 several Dutch families built farms in what is now Jersey City and Hoboken, but these immigrant settlements were periodically destroyed by Native Americans. Not until 1660 did the Dutch build a permanent fortified village, Bergen, on a hill between the Hudson and Hackensack rivers, about two miles from Manhattan.

While the Dutch settled along the Hudson, New Sweden took shape along what is today the Delaware River and Bay. Founded in 1638, New Sweden never grew beyond several hundred people, most of whom lived on what became the Pennsylvania side of the river. The settlers were Swedes and Finns. Many were convicts, "poachers, deserters from the army, debtors, and others who were in one legal difficulty or another."[1] Some, in fact, had been given the dismal choice of hanging or exile to New Sweden. The colony did not last long. In 1655 the Dutch easily captured these crude settlements and extended the area under their control up the Delaware.

English Conquest

Dutch rule in America came to an end in 1644. Four British warships entered New York harbor and without firing a shot convinced Peter Stuyvesant, the peglegged governor of New Netherland, to surrender. Control passed to James, Duke of York, brother of Charles II, King of England. He quickly transferred ownership of what is now New Jersey to Sir George Carteret and Lord John Berkeley. They became the proprietors, or owners, of the colony, exercising the rights of government as well as of land ownership. They sold off portions of their interest to different individuals, who established the separate but related provinces of East Jersey and West Jersey. The two provinces were not rejoined until 1702, when they came under royal rule.

In 1665, soon after acquiring the province, Carteret and Berkeley issued the "Concessions and Agreements" by which they set the terms of settlement for people who would locate in the province. As the proprietors could profit only by selling lands to settlers, these concessions were designed to make New Jersey an attractive place in which to settle. Among the provisions were an elected assembly, freedom of trade, and freedom of religion—but only for Protestants.

Colonial Settlers

Serious settlement of New Jersey began shortly after the beginning of the proprietors' rule. But settlement was more by migrants from New England and New Netherland than by immigrants arriving directly from abroad. Groups of English Puritans from Long Island and Connecticut migrated to New Jersey. Those from Connecticut opposed the manner in which government and religion functioned there.

Long Island migrants founded Elizabethtown in 1664. Two years later Connecticut migrants founded Newark. These settlers tended to build villages and churches very much like those they left behind, giving parts of northern New Jersey a distinctly New England look.

Dutch settlement in New Jersey actually increased after the end of Dutch rule. Migrating from the Hudson Valley and Long Island, Dutch settlers relocated along the Passaic and Raritan rivers. They carved out large farms, some of which were worked by African slave labor; they built Dutch Reformed churches and continued to speak the Dutch language. Some of these rural communities maintained their integrity for almost 250 years. While English began to replace Dutch after 1750, there were still isolated pockets in northeastern New Jersey where Dutch could be heard as late as 1900. The manner in which the rural Dutch maintained their language and culture illustrates how ethnic characteristics can be passed from one generation to another under favorable circumstances.

Settlement of West Jersey proceeded more slowly. The colony came under the control of several English Quakers in the 1670s, one of whom was William Penn. Quakers were Protestants who stressed piety, pacifism, and simplicity in both family life and religious observance. Faced with persecution in England, many preferred to abandon their homes for the uncertainties of life in the American wilderness. Between 1675 and 1681 about fourteen hundred emigrated from the British Isles to West Jersey, settling the narrow strip of land between the Delaware River and what is now known as the Pinelands near Burlington. But after Pennsylvania was founded in 1681, most arrivals chose the more fertile lands west of the Delaware. Philadelphia rather than Burlington quickly became the center of Quaker commerce and society.

By 1700 New Jersey had a population of about fifteen thousand. Two-thirds lived in East Jersey, which was populated by English Puritans who had left New England and Dutch migrants from New York's Hudson Valley. In West Jersey, English Quakers already outnumbered the original Swedish settlers. Fewer in number than the Dutch, the Swedes were less capable of remaining a distinct group. By 1800 their descendants spoke English and had joined the Anglican church. Over the course of several generations they gradually became part of the larger culture around them.

New Jersey's population increased to sixty thousand by the mid-eighteenth century and to 184,000 by 1790, the year of the first national census. Two new immigrant groups arrived in substantial numbers during that period. The smaller of the two groups consisted of Germans, mostly from the Rhineland. They tended to be Lutheran and were part of the larger German immigration into Pennsylvania. In New Jersey, however,

Germans formed few separate communities in which Germans—and German—predominated. Consequently, in New Jersey, Germans were more rapidly assimilated. By the end of the century Germans were using English even in their church services.

More numerous were the Scots-Irish. These were Irish Protestants from the north of Ireland who were descended from earlier Scots immigrants to Ireland. Because they tended to be poor, many arrived as indentured servants. This meant that they owed several years of labor to the person who paid their fare. Unlike slaves, indentured servants were free at the end of their contract obligations and could then establish their own farms.

Although most Scots-Irish settlers in America were in central Pennsylvania, west of the German communities, and further south through Virginia and North Carolina, a significant number settled in the northern half of New Jersey. Since they were English-speaking Presbyterians, they rapidly blended into colonial society and should not be considered a distinct ethnic group.

New Jersey's population grew in two other ways in the eighteenth century. First, a high birth rate meant large families. Second, a trickle of migration continued from New England and New York, swelling the numbers of those with English and Dutch backgrounds. A near wilderness in 1700, New Jersey by the American Revolution was one of the more densely populated colonies. Only the southern pine country remained unoccupied.

After the Revolution

The census taken in 1790, the first after the Revolution, reveals much about the 184,000 people living in New Jersey in that year. Just over half, 51 percent, were of English origin. When we add those from Wales, Scotland, and Ireland, including the Scots-Irish, we find that just under 70 percent traced their origin to the British Isles. Another 20 percent were of Dutch ancestry and 10 percent came from Germany and surrounding countries. By 1790 only 1 percent were of Swedish descent. The British formed a majority in all but two counties. Bergen was 53 percent Dutch and Somerset was 67 percent.

The Dutch were able to maintain a distinct and separate existence over many generations in their two counties because they were numerous and geographically concentrated.

During the next half century, from 1790 to 1840, growth was more modest. New Jersey's population merely doubled, growing to 373,000, a much slower pace than for the country as a whole. There were two reasons for the lower rate of increase. First, the best farmland had long ago been settled, and some of it had been under cultivation for 150 years. Soils were wearing thin and becoming less productive. Many people in New Jersey saw brighter opportunities further west, particularly in unspoiled areas of Pennsylvania and Ohio, and joined the great American westward migration. In 1850 at least seventy-five thousand people born in New Jersey lived west of the Delaware. New Jersey natives also moved in large numbers to New York City and Philadelphia. Between 1700 and 1840 these cities emerged as the two major commercial centers in the Middle Atlantic area. No New Jersey city would ever approach their size or rate of growth. New Jerseyans seeking to enter trade and commerce, therefore, frequently moved to one or the other. By 1850, thirty thousand New Jersey natives lived in New York City and Philadelphia.*

Second, between the Revolution and 1840 there was only a trickle of emigrants from Europe to the United States. No new immigrant groups arrived to take up residence in New Jersey. As people lived out their lives and were succeeded by their children, the population became progressively more similar in outlook and experiences. People who grew up knowing no environment other than New Jersey came to share a sense of common cultural identity. They were increasingly "American," with fewer ties to the groups and places which their immigrant ancestors had left. When large-scale immigration began again in the 1840s these descendants of immigrants would call themselves "natives." They would view the newcomers as "foreigners," as people who were all too different and who brought with them strange ways, ways that were quite inappropriate for their New Jersey.

*All population figures for the period after 1850 are taken from the published United States censuses for the appropriate years. They are not otherwise cited.

CHAPTER TWO

The "Old" Immigration, 1840–1880

The nineteenth century was a time of great economic change, in both Europe and the United States. In Europe the beginnings of industrialization and the development of large-scale, market-oriented agriculture disrupted traditional rural cultures and patterns of landholding. As a result many peasant farmers lost all hope for secure economic lives in familiar surroundings. In order to stay even, or maybe to do a little better, they had to go somewhere else. Many emigrated from the European countryside to growing European cities. Others left Europe for distant places such as Canada, South America, southern Africa, and Australia. Slightly more than half of those who left came to the United States. Immigration to this country, then, must be viewed as part of a larger population movement of Europeans to other parts of the world.

Leaving Europe

The decision to emigrate generally involved two steps. First, a person had to decide that it was necessary or desirable to leave home. Then a destination had to be carefully chosen. Usually the list of places to be considered was fairly short. Whenever possible, individuals emigrated to a place where someone they knew, either kin or neighbor, had already settled. People intending to emigrate carefully planned to link up with someone who would help in finding work and lodging. Few people sailed off into the sunset alone. Most joined relatives or villagers who had successfully gone before.

The economic changes that came with industrialization affected different parts of Europe at different times. Hence the disruptions that led to emigration came first to one area, then another. In the four decades after 1840, as the pace of emigration to the United States quickened, most arrivals came from just three places: Germany, Great Britain (which includes England, Scotland, and Wales), and Ireland. Germany and Great Britain were among the most urban and industrial areas of Europe, and most of their emigrants carried with them skills in high demand in other industrializing societies. These emigrants tended to come from the middle range of society or slightly below. The poorest could not afford the price of passage, and the prosperous seldom had strong incentives to leave.

The Irish were a case apart. For a hundred years after 1740, population increased faster than food supply, and the Irish grew slowly but steadily poorer. Most were landless agricultural laborers or tenant farmers to absentee British landlords. The poor were increasingly dependent upon the potato as the staple in their diet. In 1845 the potato crop failed, destroyed by a fungus. Ireland then began a decade of devastating famines that reduced the population by more than a third. Hundreds of thousands died of starvation or related diseases. Others fled their homeland to escape similar fates.

Many of those who left went to England, the closest and cheapest destination. Approximately 1.5 million came to the United States. The rural villagers leaving Ireland lacked the industrial skills brought by the British and Germans. Nor did they possess the capital to buy land and equip farms. Settling in American cities, Irish men found work as low-paid day laborers or on construction gangs. They often encountered what today would be called job discrimination. Newspaper want ads frequently read, "No Irish Need Apply." Yet conditions were so desperate in Ireland that almost anything was an improvement.

Arriving in New Jersey

Emigration out of Europe coincided with the beginnings of the industrial revolution in the United States. Economic growth attracted immigrants, and the arrival of new workers, in turn, quickened the pace of industrialization. Immigration, then, was both a cause and an effect of economic growth. An expanding economy provided increasing numbers of jobs at every skill level. Except in hard times even new arrivals could generally find work of some sort, if only temporary day labor. After 1840 American population growth centered increasingly on its emerging industrial cities, and the most important source of that growth was immigration from Europe.

Adjacent to ports of entry, New Jersey quickly developed a large immigrant presence. In 1860, when the nation's population was 13 percent immigrant, New Jersey's was 18 percent. Of the state's 115,000 immigrants, 50 percent were Irish, 28 percent German and 16 percent British. The remaining 6 percent came mostly from parts of northern Europe and Canada.

The state's industrial cities grew most rapidly. Newark's population increased from seventeen thousand in 1840 to seventy-two thousand in 1860. Jersey City expanded from a mere village of three thousand to a city of thirty thousand during the same period and reached 120,000 after another twenty years. Immigrants represented most of that growth. In 1860 the urban counties of Hudson, Essex, and Passaic were, respectively, 42 percent, 34 percent, and 29 percent immigrant. By contrast, the extreme southern counties of Salem, Cumberland, and Cape May averaged but 4 percent immigrant.

Jersey City's Immigrant Cultures

Jersey City in 1860 provides a graphic example of the impact of immigration on northern New Jersey's rapidly growing cities. We will look closely at the ethnic origins and occupations of that city's adult male population in order to understand how ethnicity interacted with economic class to create a particular kind of social fabric.

As Table 1 shows, by 1860 a clear majority of Jersey City's adult male population was foreign-born. The Irish were the largest group, making up over a third of the population. The British and Germans together constituted another quarter. Less than half of the inhabitants were born in the United States, and these were overwhelmingly white. Only 1 percent of the city's adult males were native-born blacks.

Table 1

Males Twenty and Over, by Ethnicity, Jersey City, 1860

	Number	Percentage
Native-born white	2818	39
Irish	2636	36
British	918	13
German	810	11
Native-born black	80	1
TOTAL	7262	100

SOURCE: Federal Manuscript Census Schedules of Jersey City, New Jersey, 1866. National Archives Microfilm Publication, Rolls 653–693. Figures computed by the author.

The relative prosperity of different ethnic groups can be gauged by the jobs in which their members clustered. Even more in 1860 than today, household income and social placement were determined primarily by the occupations of male workers. Each of Jersey City's ethnic groups had its own distinct occupational profile, different from all the others. These occupational differences led to very different patterns of poverty and prosperity. Variations in levels of poverty and prosperity in turn affected the ways these groups related to each other.

For convenience, most occupations can be grouped by skill level into the three broad categories of unskilled labor, skilled labor, and white-collar work. Unskilled workers could not earn enough to support a family and escape poverty even in good times, while skilled workers generally earned just enough to assure a minimally decent life. Men in white-collar work, on the other hand, usually earned enough to provide a very good life for themselves and their families. This group included the city's wealthiest residents, its economic elite.

Table 2 illustrates the occupational profiles of the city's four major white ethnic groups. The native-born stand out as clearly favored. A full 42 percent were in occupations that may have provided at least a middle-class income and in many cases probably offered wealth. Another third were skilled workers. Only 9 percent of the native-born were unskilled laborers.

The Irish were at the other extreme. Well over half were among the working poor, and it is hardly possible to talk about an Irish middle or upper class. Having recently immigrated and generally lacking industrial skills, most of the Irish eked out a bare existence with few comforts and no margin for times

Table 2

White Males Twenty and Over, by Ethnicity and Occupation, Jersey City, 1860

	Native		Irish		British		German	
	Number	Percentage	Number	Percentage	Number	Percentage	Number	Percentage
White-collar	1,180	42	168	7	236	26	110	14
Skilled	969	34	743	28	498	54	482	60
Unskilled	254	9	1,472	56	106	12	109	13
Other*	415	15	235	9	78	8	109	13
TOTAL	2,818	100	2,618	100	918	100	810	100

*The "Other" category includes those who listed no occupation (many of whom were over 60) or whose occupation did not readily fit into a classification based on skill.

SOURCE: Federal Manuscript Census Schedules of Jersey City, New Jersey, 1860. National Archives Microfilm Publication, Rolls 653–693. Figures computed by the author.

of adversity. Over 75 percent of the unskilled laborers in Jersey City were Irish. When the native-born complained that the poor were Irish and the Irish were poor, they were not far from the mark.

Language aside, the British and Germans shared much in common with each other. Coming from urban and industrial backgrounds, they were able to command better wages in skilled work. Neither group contained large numbers of unskilled poor, and each had a fair number who could be counted as middle class. Both were less well situated than the native-born, but in far better circumstances than the Irish. Generally speaking, British and German families could provide for themselves in a spare but satisfactory manner.

To supplement the low wages paid to male laborers, poor families commonly relied on the additional earnings of other household members, usually women and children. But opportunities were few and pay was poor. Married women almost never worked outside the home. They were more likely to take in boarders, extending their household space and services to those who would pay for room, meals, and laundry. Even unmarried women seldom worked outside a household setting. They tended to find employment either as live-in domestic servants or as seamstresses or dressmakers working in their own homes.

Whether women worked before marriage related directly to the economic circumstances of their families. Immigrant women worked much more frequently than native-born ones, and Irish women were more likely to work than all others. Indeed, few Irish women escaped working for wages at some point between adolescence and marriage. By age twenty nearly half of all Irish women had left their parents' homes to work in other households as domestic servants. Native middle-class households employed about 80 percent of the city's servants. Servants' wages often went to help support parents, brothers, and sisters elsewhere in the city.

Whether or not women worked, either in their own or someone else's household, then, related directly to the income of husbands and fathers. Class and ethnicity intersected. While few native-born women worked for wages, most Irish women did at some point in their lives, a direct consequence of the low incomes of Irish males.

Jersey City was hardly unique. The same population patterns characterized Newark, Paterson, Trenton, and other industrial cities. Proportions sometimes differed. Hoboken and Newark were more heavily German than Jersey City. But almost everywhere immigrants constituted a majority of the urban adult populations, making cities very different from the surrounding countryside. British and German immigrants commonly clustered in the skilled trades, while the Irish worked mostly as unskilled laborers. The native-born controlled the most lucrative opportunities and owned most of the wealth and property. As a result they were able to dominate many aspects of society, even when they were not in the majority.

Ethnic Tensions

Immigration created a society that was both increasingly diverse and increasingly uncomfortable with that diversity. Today we celebrate American pluralism, our self-proclaimed ability to harmonize divergent cultures with minimal discord. Nineteenth-century Americans did not seek or value pluralism. Instead they labeled many of the religious beliefs and social practices that immigrants brought with them as threats to "American" values and culture.

Since the Reformation in the sixteenth century, European Protestants and Catholics had distrusted and disliked each other. Between 1500 and 1800, Europeans went to war on several occasions over religious issues. In Protestant nations, Catholics were viewed as potential subversives, as were Protestants in Catholic nations.

Protestant English colonists brought their suspicions and fears to America. Their nineteenth-century descendants, schooled in these traditions, viewed the Catholic Church as an alien force that threatened the foundations of religious freedom and democratic order. A New Jersey Dutch Reformed minister wrote in the 1850s that Catholicism was "subversive alike of civil liberty, freedom of conscience, and the purity of Religion."[1] Until 1844 the New Jersey state constitution allowed only Protestants to hold public office.

A second challenge came from the European preference for what native-born Americans called the "Continental Sabbath."

This was a set of customs which treated Sunday more as a secular holiday than as a time for religious observance and quiet contemplation. Many immigrants used their only day without labor for the enjoyment of sports, games, secular music, and visits to European-style beer gardens.

Americans considered these immigrant customs a grave threat to social order. They were determined to maintain the explicitly Protestant tilt of the country's institutional structure and to force a quiet American "Christian" Sabbath on everyone, regardless of preference. Germans in particular resented American demands that they give up their traditional amusements and take up more serious and sober pursuits. Culture clashed with culture as Irish and German immigrants resisted assaults on cherished religious beliefs and familiar secular customs.

To understand why the native-born felt so severely threatened in their own land, we must look again at the ethnic and occupational structures of New Jersey's industrial cities. In our example, Jersey City, the two groups that differed most sharply from each other were the predominantly middle-class native-born and the predominantly unskilled Irish. They were also the two largest groups in the city, together accounting for 75 percent of the adult males and their families. They differed in cultural origins, in what they did for a living, in income and lifestyle, and, most important, in religion.

It was the large number of differences separating the native-born from the Irish that sustained ethnic tensions. It is hardly surprising that people who differed in so many ways were unable to find many issues on which they shared a common perspective or to sympathize with each other's views and practices.

Native Fears

In February 1853, New Brunswick school reformer David Bishop received an invitation from a Newark chapter of the Order of United Americans (O.U.A.) to attend a George Washington's birthday commemoration at the Halsey Street Methodist Church in Newark. The O.U.A. was one of several semisecret fraternal societies dedicated to keeping American culture free from foreign influence. It was active and fairly successful in New Jersey in the 1850s. The Native American, or "Know-Nothing," political party* grew out of these nativist organizations.

To call attention to that which was uniquely American, O.U.A. chapters publicly celebrated George Washington's birthday. As the number of European immigrants rose, this celebration took on increasing symbolic importance for the native-born. It was "their" day. That the chapter which invited David Bishop planned to hold its meeting in a Protestant church illustrates how the country's Protestant tradition helped shape important aspects of American nationalism.

David Bishop could not attend the celebration and sent his regrets. His letter listed what he believed to be the duties of native-born Americans in an era of change and stress:

1st. To thwart the "insidious evils" of papal aggression upon American Schools and American Laws.

2nd. To rescue our Sabbaths and [liquor] Laws from the impudence and contempt of German infidelity.

3rd. To see to it that the Irish reverence our statutes and pay their taxes.

4th. To make [secure] the livelihood and comfort of the native and naturalized mechanic† against all foreign competition whatever.[2]

Here, in summary order, was the agenda for New Jersey's nativists.

Anti-Catholicism

To many nineteenth-century Americans, Catholicism was intimately linked with European autocratic governments, enemies of democratic institutions. Catholicism represented both a re-

---

*Members of the O.U.A. were instructed to say "I know nothing" when asked about the organization by outsiders. Hence they were derisively called "Know-Nothings" by their opponents. The name stuck, and is still used to refer both to members of the order and to the associated political party.

†Before the twentieth century, the term "mechanic" was used to refer to almost any skilled manual worker. Carpenters, wagon makers, and blacksmiths were all mechanics.

ligious and a political threat to the nation. Charles Deshler of New Brunswick, one of the New Jersey organizers of the O.U.A., told a group of supporters in a George Washington's birthday address, *"we* are the children of the men who [joined together] the Protestant religion and the liberties of America." Hence, "Protestantism and Republicanism are indissolubly linked together."[3]

Nowhere was this link stronger than in the curriculum of the public schools. Students learned their history from a Protestant point of view and used the Protestant Bible as a text. Some Protestants thought that the public schools should work actively to convert Catholic children. As Catholics became more numerous in New Jersey they objected to such teaching. When their objections were ignored, many withdrew their children from the public schools in favor of newly established parochial schools.

During the 1850s Catholics in several cities requested a share of local school-tax revenue to support their schools. They argued that their schools, like the public schools, performed a necessary public service and that Catholics paid school taxes from which they did not benefit. Alarmed Protestants successfully prevented such appropriations. They considered government support for Catholic education a subversion of American ideals.

The theme of potential subversion through Catholic power recurred frequently. New Jersey Governor William Newell expressed it in his annual message to the legislature in 1860. "When [Irish Catholic] mysticism and [German] infidelity shall come to predominate over the faith of our fathers, we may expect anarchy and civil war to follow." Such "innovations," he continued, would eventually "destroy our national characteristics, and silently prepare the way for subverting our religion and our government."[4]

With this stark vision of the future before them, Protestants created numerous organizations designed to convert Irish Catholics and German freethinkers to American Protestantism. In all major cities in the state, local chapters of the American Bible Society attempted to provide each Catholic family with a Protestant Bible. In Jersey City and Newark, local mission and tract societies attempted to visit each family monthly, especially in poor and immigrant neighborhoods, and leave a piece of Protestant literature. Such efforts, however, resulted in few conversions and were largely discontinued after the Civil War.

Local governments also aided Protestant efforts. In Jersey City's almshouse, its shelter for the destitute and homeless, the overseer of the poor required all children to attend weekly religious services and strongly urged adults to attend as well. Some adult inmates claimed that refusal brought physical abuse. The services were "unsectarian," with various Protestant ministers preaching to all inmates regardless of their religious preference.

In 1857 and again in 1862 prominent Jersey City Catholics petitioned the city council to allow a priest to minister to the exclusive needs of Catholics, who constituted about 80 percent of the almshouse residents, and to exempt Catholic children from Protestant preaching. Each time the council rejected the complaints. They would allow priests to do only what the city's Protestant clergy did, conducting general "unsectarian" services for all inmates. They would not allow "sectarian" services exclusively for Catholic believers. Catholics grumbled bitterly that the city showed "dishonest fanaticism" as well as a desire "to proselytize the Catholic children of the poor."[5]

Sometimes tensions spilled over into the streets. Protestant youths taunted the Irish by hanging "Paddy" in effigy, complete with whiskey bottle and potato necklace. Catholic youths occasionally disrupted Protestant services, especially when anti-Catholic preachers occupied the pulpit.

A major riot erupted in Newark in 1854 which resulted in the looting of a Catholic church and the death of an Irish Catholic laborer. It began when a procession of Irish Protestant societies entered a Catholic area. Arguments and then fistfights broke out between marchers and onlookers. Finally the marchers, some of whom were armed, broke ranks and sacked St. Mary's Catholic Church. Pistol shots killed one Irish Catholic and wounded several more. Only police intervention prevented the mob from torching the church.

Economic Nativism

Economic issues also contributed to nativism. Native-born workers feared that the flood of immigrants desperate for work would drag down wages. Then native workers' own standard of living would fall from American to European levels as too many workers competed for too few jobs. Workers and their supporters argued that only by limiting immigration could American labor receive protection from unfair and undeserved foreign competition.

Yet the nativist belief that immigrants were harmful to American culture and living standards coexisted uneasily with the conviction that the nation was and ought to be a refuge for the oppressed of other lands. Further, Americans were aware of the fact that their country was largely unsettled and that additional people were required to sustain development. Hence while nativists in the nineteenth century tended to protest the impact of immigrants on certain aspects of American culture, they seldom sought to solve their problems by closing the door to new arrivals. That solution would not find acceptance until after World War I. Instead, they worked to modify beliefs and regulate behavior, to change others without being changed themselves. Assimilation was never meant to be a two-way street.

Immigrant Cultures

When immigrants arrived in New Jersey cities, they immediately set out to reestablish as much of their old lives as their new environment would permit. For British immigrants this was an easy task. The culture they entered was quite similar to the one they left. Hence the British felt little need to create organizations that would help preserve specific aspects of a British way of life.

For others the task was more difficult. Roman Catholic immigrants entering a distinctly Protestant culture made the parish church a focal point of community life. In addition to its religious functions, the church served as a place where language and customs could be maintained and preserved. But this necessitated some changes in traditional church organization.

In Europe a parish was a geographical area with all residents attending one church. In the United States, however, Catholics with different languages and customs inhabited the same space and found it difficult to share a church and a priest without conflict. To avoid these problems, the American Catholic

People left Europe for many reasons. This cartoon lists some of them. It also suggests some of the ambiguity in the welcome immigrants received. Note the pointed caricatures of various immigrant "types" and the sarcastic last item ("Free LUNCH") on the sign next to Uncle Sam. Courtesy NEW-YORK HISTORICAL SOCIETY *and* PICTURE COLLECTION, BRANCH LIBRARIES, NEW YORK PUBLIC LIBRARY.

Church developed a system of national parishes with each immigrant group having its own set of churches and parish boundaries. In this way Irish Catholics could be Irish as well as Catholic. German Catholics could maintain German religious traditions and use the church community to preserve the German language. Catholic churches to this day are often associated with the immigrant group which constituted their first communicants.

After religion, immigrants worked to preserve their language and literary traditions. Both Catholic and Protestant Germans worshipped in German and created numerous German-language singing and literary societies. While English was useful for communicating with non-Germans, German remained the language of home and neighborhood. Parents raised their children in the same tradition. Private German-language schools flourished in every major city. Where Germans were particularly numerous, as in Hoboken, they were often able to persuade school boards to establish German-language public schools. Language helped to bind an ethnic group together and allow it to maintain its traditions.

Indeed, some Irish commentators explained the greater prosperity of the Germans by emphasizing the way a separate language built German consciousness and unity. They urged the Irish to revive Gaelic, the ancient language of Ireland, as a means of improving their lot in the United States. In the 1870s every major New Jersey city had at least one Gaelic school where small numbers of Irish sought to achieve a more secure place in American society not by assimilation but by setting themselves further apart. A Hoboken resident wrote that learning Gaelic "means you will feel more proud and manly as Irishmen, and be more respected as American citizens."[6]

Gaelic, however, never became the bond that unified the Irish. Much more important was Irish nationalism, the burning desire of the Irish to free their native land from hated British rule. In the 1860s New Jersey's Irish gave support to the Fenian Brotherhood. The Fenians wanted to free Ireland by force of arms. After the American Civil War they tried to invade British Canada with the intent of holding it hostage in return for Irish freedom. The invasion was a failure. Later, in the 1880s, Irish laborers and servants contributed to the Irish National Land League from their meager earnings. This organization worked to limit the power of British landlords in Ireland and to improve the lives of the Irish rural poor.

Nationalist activity involved the Irish in a collective unifying enterprise. Sometimes those experiences carried over into other aspects of life. The two most important strike leaders in an 1882 Jersey City dock strike, P. J. O'Sullivan and Jeremiah Murphy, were both Irish-born, and in Ireland both had actively opposed British rule. In fact, each had emigrated to avoid imprisonment and then had continued to support the nationalist cause in the

United States. Their commitment and skills as labor leaders in New Jersey grew directly out of their involvement in Irish nationalism.

The same was true for Joseph McDonnell. Emigrating to Paterson after serving three terms in British prisons for nationalist activity, McDonnell founded the Paterson Labor Standard, a radical newspaper. Through his paper and other activities, McDonnell worked to improve the lives of Paterson's working poor. Among his accomplishments was the founding of the New Jersey Federation of Trades and Labor Unions. In 1884 he became a state inspector of factories and work places, monitoring workplace safety. The perspective he acquired as a nationalist in Ireland helped shape his approach to injustice and inequality in America.

Combating Nativism: Victories and Defeats

As New Jersey's immigrant communities grew, their members found certain aspects of native culture in conflict with their own sense of justice and right. Most Europeans found American attitudes towards Sunday behavior and alcoholic beverages particularly bewildering and unnecessarily severe. But law enforcement and judicial institutions remained firmly in the hands of native-born Protestants. They used the police and the courts to suppress Sunday drinking and to deal harshly with public drunkenness, especially among the immigrant poor. Only as Irish and German immigrants became citizens and voters were they able to challenge the native-born. Conflicts over these issues lasted from the 1850s until well into the twentieth century. As we are seeing with the current debates on abortion and school prayer, conflicts over moral issues tend to be long-lasting and not readily compromised.

Jersey City provides insights into the tensions caused by competing views of what constituted a proper moral order. In 1860, although 60 percent of Jersey City's population was immigrant, virtually all elected and appointed office holders were native-born. The city judge who dealt with minor offenses was a staunch Protestant and temperance advocate. The long sentences and demeaning lectures he gave to those charged with alcohol and Sabbath offenses offended many immigrants.

In 1861 Irish and German elements in the Democratic party

forced the nomination of a more tolerant and secular candidate and worked successfully for his election. The following year the same coalition replaced a nativist police chief (the office was elective) with an Irish Catholic who increased the number of Irish patrolmen on the force. By mid-decade Jersey City's police and courts were much more sympathetic to the "Continental" Sabbath and its customs.

Similar changes took place elsewhere in city government. The number of elected aldermen who were immigrants or the sons of immigrants slowly rose. By 1869 fewer than 30 percent of the aldermen were native-born Protestants of native parentage. The immigrant aldermen tended to respond to the concerns of their immigrant constituents. They supported striking machinists in a dispute with the Erie Railroad and showed little enthusiasm for enforcing a "Christian" Sabbath. They supported Irish nationalism by allowing local Irish military companies to drill in the city armory, and by appropriating money to celebrate the arrival of visiting revolutionaries from Ireland.

This was not a situation which Jersey City's native Protestants were willing to accept. In 1871 they wrote a new city charter designed to restore their power. Approved and imposed by the state legislature, the new charter transferred many government functions from the elected board of aldermen to commissions appointed directly by the legislature itself. The legislators, most of whom were native-born and rural, ensured that each commission was securely controlled by native-born Protestants.

In addition, the charter specified new boundaries for city election districts. These lines were drawn to favor the native-born and to limit Irish influence. As many Irish voters as possible were crammed into one large crescent-shaped district, soon known throughout the state as "The Horseshoe." The native-born regained control of Jersey City by changing the rules. The new government served its creators as expected. It dismissed many Irish police officers and once again enforced the Sunday drinking laws.

While similar controversies affected other New Jersey cities, nowhere else did the defenders of the old order resort to such extreme measures. Newark's Law and Order League strove to keep that city dry on Sundays, but Newark's immigrant voters frustrated their best efforts as often as not by electing the "wrong" people to public office.

Catholic concern with the Protestant orientation of schools and other state institutions again became an issue in the mid-1870s. Catholic interests petitioned the legislature for a reformatory to be funded by the state but administered by the Church. An intense Protestant backlash across the state assured the measure's defeat. The following year an aroused electorate voted overwhelmingly to approve an amendment to the New Jersey constitution that banned any future state appropriations to schools or other institutions run by religious societies.

A New Generation

By 1880 the men and women of the "old" immigration were indeed growing older. Many had been in the country for a generation and had raised their American-born children to adulthood. These children were now entering American society on their own. While they were not immigrants, they had matured in immigrant households and neighborhoods. They had absorbed important aspects of their parents' beliefs and practices. They were ethnics rather than immigrants. As the second generation, they would constitute an increasingly important segment of New Jersey's "old" immigrant communities in the decades to come.

CHAPTER THREE

The "New" Immigration, 1880–1920

After 1880 most immigrants to the United States came from a different group of lands. Year by year the percentage of Irish, British, and Germans began to drop as conditions in those countries became more settled. At the same time, immigration from southern and eastern Europe—from Italy, Poland, Russia, and the Austro-Hungarian Empire—began to rise. These groups are known collectively as the "new" immigration, to distinguish them from the western Europeans who dominated immigration before 1880.

People emigrated from these areas to escape the dislocation that accompanied population growth and rapid economic change. As in Germany and Great Britain half a century before, urbanization and industrialization placed traditional village society under stress. Commercial agriculture began to displace peasant agriculture, threatening the livelihood of small landowners. These dislocations forced people off the land, often into nearby towns. Some stopped there. Others migrated to more distant industrial centers, and some eventually left Europe entirely, usually for the United States.

Emigrants left with a variety of goals and hopes for their futures. Some brought their families, intending never to return. Others, especially single males, viewed life in America as a temporary sojourn. They intended to work hard for good wages, save, and return with enough money to establish themselves more securely at home. Those who emigrated tended to be above the poorest classes. They also tended to be younger, healthier, and more skilled than those who stayed behind. They were hardly "the dregs of Europe" as their detractors in the United States proclaimed.

One group could not return. Eastern European Jews from Russia, Poland, and Rumania fled religious and political persecution and economic oppression. Between 1880 and 1914, a full third of all eastern European Jews left their homelands, often driven out by bloody anti-Semitic violence. Like the Irish, Jews gave their support to the creation of an independent national state. The Irish Free State came into existence in 1921. Israel followed in 1948. Immigrants to America helped found both.

Crossing the Atlantic

By the time of the new immigration, trans-Atlantic travel had made the transition from sail to steam. This cut the time and expense of the journey while improving safety and comfort. Yet

Immigrant ships were crowded and unpleasant. The accommodations on
this ship, which was on its way to Australia from England in the 1840s,
were similar to those on North Atlantic ships throughout the century.
Courtesy PICTURE COLLECTION, BRANCH LIBRARIES, NEW YORK PUBLIC
LIBRARY.

for emigrants in steerage, a sort of bulk-rate packaging of
human beings for delivery to America, conditions were harsh
enough. Multilevel wooden bunks in windowless holds, poor
food, and few sanitary facilities were all a part of steerage. One
emigrant graphically described an outbreak of seasickness in a
crowded steerage compartment:

> As all were crossing the ocean for the first time, they thought
> their end had come.... [No] sooner had I thrust my head
> forward from the lower bunk than someone above me vomited
> straight upon my head. I wiped the vomit away, dragged myself
> onto the deck, leaned against the railing and vomited my share
> into the sea, and lay down half-dead upon the deck.[1]

Arrival in New Jersey

After the rigors of the voyage, immigrants landed at Ellis
Island in New York harbor. There they were questioned,
processed, inspected for disease, and finally admitted to the
country. As in earlier years, a disproportionate number settled
in New Jersey. Between 1880 and 1920 immigrants from
southern and eastern Europe once again changed the nature

Immigrants bound for New Jersey landed first at Ellis Island in New York harbor. Courtesy NATIONAL PARK SERVICE, STATUE OF LIBERTY NATIONAL MONUMENT/ELLIS ISLAND MUSEUM OF IMMIGRATION.

of the state's population. Between 1880 and 1910 the proportion of immigrants in New Jersey's population rose from 20 percent to 26 percent. Then World War I disrupted immigration and the figure fell back to 23 percent in 1920.

But that was not the whole story. In 1920 another 34 percent of the state's population were the children of immigrants. Only 38 percent—less than two-fifths—were native-born whites of native-born parents. More than 60 percent were either immigrant or second generation. New Jersey was truly an ethnic state.*

As New Jersey became increasingly immigrant, its population became increasingly diverse. The impact of the "new" immigra-

*The census recorded 3.8 percent of the population as nonwhite: Negroes (3.75 percent) and Asians (0.05 percent).

tion can be appreciated by comparing the state's largest immigrant groups in 1880 with those in 1920, as shown in Table 3. While the British, Irish, and Germans dominated in 1880, they were much less prominent forty years later. Italians constituted by far the largest group and Poles were third. Members of the new immigration made up a clear majority (62 percent) of those groups listed in Table 3.

Immigrants settling in New Jersey entered a dynamic economy with an expanding industrial base and a constant demand for skilled and unskilled labor. They found work in the steel, tobacco, and pencil factories of Jersey City; in the leather and textile works of Newark; in the silk mills of Paterson; and in the potteries of Trenton. They laid railroad and streetcar track, dug the water and sewer ditches required by booming cities, and unloaded freight from railroad cars, canal boats, barges, and steamers.

Few who were physically fit were out of work for long, but they rarely found jobs that supported more than basic existence. Immigrants from Poland and Italy gradually displaced the Irish at unskilled labor. While unskilled work might support a single male, it was not adequate for a family; to assure survival families relied on more than one income. Wives seldom worked outside the home but did "piecework" or took in paying boarders. Children entered the workforce in their early teens, with boys often assisting fathers as helpers. Family earnings were pooled for collective support, and the years of greatest family prosperity generally came when the number of incomes was at its peak.

The Second Generation

By 1880 a generation of children born in America to members of the "old" immigration had come of age. They were both Americans and part of an immigrant culture. Their ethnic identities were important parts of their personalities and helped shape the way they approached life in the United States. Almost all retained the religion of their parents. Yet their sense of membership in European cultures was less strong, part of a heritage rather than a living memory.

Generally speaking, those in the second generation held better jobs than their parents. They were more educated and more

Table 3

Place of Origin, Major Immigrant Groups, New Jersey, 1880 and 1920

Place	1880		1920	
	Number	Percentage	Number	Percentage
1. Ireland / 1. Italy*	93,079	42.0	157,285	21.3
2. Germany / 2. Germany	64,935	29.3	92,382	12.5
3. Great Britain / 3. Poland*	39,803	18.0	90,419	12.2
4. Holland / 4. Russia*	4,281	1.9	73,527	10.0
5. France / 5. Ireland	3,739	1.7	65,971	8.9
6. Canada / 6. Great Britain	3,536	1.6	65,817	8.9
Other / 7. Hungary*	12,327	5.5	40,470	5.5
TOTAL / 8. Austria*	221,700	100.0	36,917	5.0
9. Czechoslovakia*			16,747	2.3
10. Holland			12,737	1.7
11. Canada			10,292	1.4
12. France			10,185	1.4
Other			65,864	8.9
TOTAL			738,613	100.0

*"New" immigrants

SOURCE: Adapted from United States Census, 1880, Table 14, and United States Census, 1920, New Jersey, Table 12.

Children of immigrant parents frequently entered the factories at an early age. This boy is at work in the Clark Thread Mills in Paterson. Courtesy AMERICAN LABOR MUSEUM, BOTTO HOUSE NATIONAL LANDMARK.

likely to have valuable skills. Also, as later immigrants expanded both the economy and the base of the occupational structure, those already here were in the best position to take advantage of new opportunities above the level of unskilled labor. Thus the "new" immigrants, just by arriving, helped to create a more favorable economic environment for the children of the "old" immigration.

To see how the second generation fared, we shall look briefly at Jersey City's "Horseshoe" district in 1880. This was one of the most heavily immigrant areas in New Jersey, and also one of the poorest. Immigrants and their children made up 86 percent of the Horseshoe's adult male population. Those of Irish birth or parentage constituted 63 percent. Among the Irish-born, 68 percent were unskilled. But only 47 percent of the American-born children of Irish parents were unskilled. Just 20 percent of the Irish-born were in skilled trades, compared to 36 percent of their children. Similar patterns characterized the German population. While immigrants worked disproportionately at low-paying jobs, the second generation did better. The promise of America typically included a more prosperous and secure life for one's children.

Italians in Newark

The Italians in Newark provide a good case study of the state's "new" immigrants. Between 1880 and 1920 Newark's Italian-born population grew from four hundred to twenty-seven thousand. By the latter date another thirty-six thousand were the children of Italian parents. Those of Italian birth and parentage made up 15 percent of the city's population, and had become Newark's largest ethnic group.

Most had emigrated from the declining agricultural regions of southern Italy and Sicily. Whenever possible, people from the same village settled near each other. "Each town in Italy," one observer wrote, "had its counterpart on a street in some part of New Jersey."[2] Italian immigrants attempted to transfer as much of village life as they could. Back home each village had a patron saint. In Newark, villagers established societies to honor those saints. Italian social and religious life revolved around these societies. Their annual feasts and parades involved months of preparation which culminated in festivities lasting up to five days. Mutual aid societies, also organized on village lines, complemented the religious societies and provided insurance against medical and funeral expenses.

In spite of local attachments, life in Newark forced Italians from different regions to live close together. While they could be found in all parts of the city in 1920, over half lived in just three of Newark's sixteen wards. Over 80 percent of the First Ward's foreign-born were Italian. This type of clustering was not unusual. Eastern European Jews clustered in the Third Ward, while half of all Lithuanians lived in the Tenth. Three-quarters of the small Portuguese community resided in the Fourth. New arrivals sought the security of others like themselves.

Ethnic clustering created ethnic neighborhoods. Here immigrants could continue familiar customs and ways. In Newark's

Italian immigrants arrived with much hope and few possessions. This family is on its way to Ellis Island. Courtesy LEWIS W. HINE COLLECTION, U.S. HISTORY, LOCAL HISTORY AND GENEALOGY DIVISION, NEW YORK PUBLIC LIBRARY, ASTOR, LENOX AND TILDEN FOUNDATIONS.

crowded First Ward, Italian immigrants could deal only with other Italians and satisfy all their daily needs. Boarding houses catered to new arrivals from Italy, easing their entry into American society. Street vendors with pushcarts or horse-drawn wagons sold fruits and vegetables. Small groceries occupied the ground floors of corner tenements. One observer in the 1930s wrote of their "cheeses, garlic, salami and red pepper hanging from the rafters, . . . over 150 different types of macaroni," and "olive oil, imported and domestic, in all price ranges."[3]

As immigrant communities grew, the number of situations requiring contact with members outside the community diminished. The variety of goods and services that could be purchased from fellow immigrants increased to include almost all normal demands. For this reason, immigrants living in large ethnic communities tended to enter the mainstream of English-speaking society more slowly. In Newark's First Ward, for example, a knowledge of English was unnecessary for tending to the needs of daily existence.

Italians generally supported that existence by the sweat of unskilled labor. By 1890 half of the laborers who maintained the railroad tracks between New York and Philadelphia were Italian, rapidly replacing the Irish. "Industry in New Jersey," one historian has written, "developed a rough caste system in which ethnic origin largely determined one's position in the occupational hierarchy."[4] At the top, as owners and managers, were native white Americans. In the middle, as foremen and skilled workers, were Irish, German, and British. Increasingly, Italians and eastern Europeans were at the bottom.

Italian laborers commonly worked in gangs organized by Italian *padrones* who contracted for the group and paid their men a portion of what they received. Typically, a *padrone* spoke English and Italian. He functioned as the link between American bosses and Italian workers. A railroad rebuilding its track

These Italian construction workers are at work in Morristown, probably in the 1920s. Courtesy JAMES COSTANZO and MORRIS COUNTY HISTORICAL SOCIETY.

through the Newark meadows hired fifty *padrones*. Each one collected about a hundred laborers and took 4 percent of each one's wage. While the *padrone* system often involved abuses and exploitation, it did provide the means for non-English-speaking laborers to get work quickly.

A few Italians achieved real economic success. Vito Marzano opened a clothing shop in Newark in 1885. He was trusted by his customers, who often deposited money with him for safekeeping. The banking side of his business slowly grew. In 1925 he incorporated the Marzano State Bank, later the Bank of Commerce. But success usually was more modest, no more than a small shop. Italians came to dominate Newark's barbering and shoe repair trades, and Italian bakeries dotted the city.

Italians met considerable discrimination outside their community. Skilled and unskilled workers feared that competition from Italian and eastern European immigrants would force wages down. Native Protestants viewed Italians as rude and barely civilized, unfit for white-collar work regardless of formal qualifications. Even professionals were suspect. Doctors and dentists with Italian names seldom built successful practices outside Italian neighborhoods. Ethnic stereotypes restricted Italian opportunities, as was the case with "new" immigrants generally.

Nor did Italians fit neatly into the American Catholic church. Italian Catholicism clashed with the austere practices of the dominant Irish. Italians placed greater emphasis on the intercession of saints, and they mixed formal religion with ancient beliefs in a world of good and evil spirits. Newark's Italians strove to establish their own "nationality" parishes, erecting five churches between 1887 and 1925. These were staffed by Italian-born priests who maintained the language and customs of southern Italy. Italians, then, found ethnic tensions inside the church as well as in secular society.

As with religion, Italians arrived with strong convictions about how families should function. They modified their behavior only enough to adjust to a new setting. In Italy, for example, Italians married late and averaged about five children per family. Female children lived under strict parental control and parents often arranged their children's marriages. In America, arranged marriages were rare and couples married younger. Yet Italians continued to have large families by American standards and to insist that children live in the family until marriage. In spite of the need for multiple incomes, unmarried Italian women were much less likely to work outside the home than women from other ethnic groups.

Rural Jewish Settlements

Although most immigrants had to live in industrial cities, some were able to realize agricultural ideals. In 1882 the Hebrew Emigrant Aid Society organized Alliance, a farming colony in southern New Jersey for newly arrived Russian Jews. Alliance was the first of several such settlements financed by wealthy Jews from New York and Philadelphia. Their goal was to help fellow Jews escape the crowding and disease of the industrial centers. But life on the poor soils of southern New Jersey was hard, and success came slowly. Rural Jewish colonies attracted attention and comment, but involved relatively few people. In 1920 only a small percentage of New Jersey's Jewish population lived on farms.

Laborers in Cities

The upper limits of immigrant concentration were reached in the city of Passaic. In 1920 85 percent of Passaic's adult population was what the census termed "foreign stock"— foreign-born or of foreign parentage. In the First Ward 99 percent of the population was foreign stock. Fewer than one hundred (seventy-two whites, twenty-three blacks) out of 10,365 adults could claim parents born in the United States.

Passaic's immigrants, attracted by the city's numerous textile mills, were mostly eastern Europeans. Two-thirds came from Poland, Hungary, Russia, Austria, and Czechoslovakia. They were generally poor and lived under extremely crowded conditions. Only the river wards of Hoboken and Jersey City had more families per dwelling than Passaic's First Ward. More than one in five immigrant adults in Passaic were illiterate, compared to less than one in a hundred among the native-born. Low wages and irregular work contributed to poverty and discontent. Mill owners fiercely resisted worker attempts at organization. Between 1875 and 1926 several major strikes convulsed the community as Passaic's immigrant workers tried with little success to improve their wages and working conditions.

Immigrants in other cities also organized to improve their lot. In 1913 the militant Industrial Workers of the World led twenty-five thousand Paterson textile operatives through a bitter five-month strike. The mill owners refused to negotiate. Alarmed by radical I.W.W. rhetoric, Paterson's largely native-born business community came together behind the owners. Police arrested strike leaders on trumped-up charges and forbade speeches by "out-of-town agitators." As one scholar puts it, the mill owners regarded their immigrant employees "quite simply as unworthy of any consideration, not really 'people' at all."[5] Consequently they saw no reason to respect even the most basic of American civil liberties.

A similar event occurred in 1915 at Standard Oil's huge refinery complex in Bayonne. Much of the work was hot, dirty,

Immigrant weavers march in the 1913 Paterson textile strike. Courtesy COLLECTIONS OF THE PASSAIC COUNTY HISTORICAL SOCIETY, PATERSON, N.J.

and dangerous, with the worst tasks assigned to immigrants. To obstruct union organization the company consciously created work groups out of people who spoke different languages. Nevertheless, the workers, who were predominantly Polish, struck for higher wages, better working conditions, and an end to abuse by Irish foremen. To crush the strike, the refinery's manager brought in Italian strikebreakers and called for "two hundred and fifty husky men who can swing clubs" to march "through the guts of Polacks."[6] The strike ended after the county sheriff made a patriotic appeal to the few native-born workers and convinced them to return to work. Demoralized, the rest followed.

Nativism

To New Jersey's native-born middle class, cities like Passaic, Paterson, and Bayonne were indeed fearsome places. Like their parents and grandparents, they felt threatened by cultural and religious diversity. The poverty, illiteracy, and labor militancy of the "new" immigrants heightened their alarm. Raised in the traditions of pre–Civil War nativism, they adapted those traditions to the problems and dislocations of their age.

Anti-Catholicism continued as the dominant nativist theme through the 1880s. Native Protestants continued to oppose state support to church schools and to enforce Bible reading in the public schools. They still considered the United States to be "their" country and worked to prevent what they called "sectarian" influences. Catholics, frustrated by the Protestant tilt of state and school, continued to create separate institutions.

Protestants also worked to limit access to alcohol and to preserve the "Christian" Sabbath. Of particular concern was the urban saloon, patronized by immigrants. Every session of New Jersey's legislature considered "the liquor question" anew. For example, in 1888 the legislators passed a law that sharply raised the annual fee for liquor licenses in large cities and increased the penalities for Sunday sales. But this act, like others, was soon repealed. As every possible policy outraged significant portions of the state's population, "the liquor question" remained a continuous open controversy. Indeed, some aspects have never been resolved.

After 1890 two new themes became increasingly important in American nativism. One was loosely based on an incorrect interpretation of Charles Darwin's theories of evolution and natural selection. The "races" of southern and eastern Europe were held to be inferior to those of Anglo-Saxon origin. They were supposed to lack the Anglo-Saxon gift for democratic self-government and therefore to be incapable of assimilation. Hence to permit large numbers to immigrate threatened national stability. These arguments helped fuel the movement for immigration restriction, which gained strength in the early twentieth century.

The second theme concerned immigrant political radicalism. The native-born blamed most labor discontent on "foreign" political and economic ideologies imported by immigrants. They felt particularly threatened by Socialists, who rejected private ownership of profit-making property, and Anarchists, who rejected most government. Strikes and other disorders were often blamed on them. Anarchists and Socialists were also condemned for questioning the basic fairness of the economic system and the distribution of wealth and income.

Protecting the country's governmental and economic systems from European radicalism became a prime nativist objective. Related to these concerns was a conviction that many immigrants arrived with criminal tendencies and were prone to violence. These two images merged into a stereotype of immigrants as law-breaking revolutionaries who threatened the stability of the Republic and its institutions.

To counter these threats many native Protestants joined patriotic fraternal societies. The two most important in New Jersey were the Junior Order United American Mechanics (O.U.A.M.) and the Patriotic Sons of America. Before 1880 they worked mostly to limit Catholic influence. In later years combatting radicalism became more important. The Patriotic Sons of America watched New Jersey's cities fill with "anarchists and dynamiters," people "who love the red flag better and more than they do the stars and stripes," and feared for the future.[7]

Patriotic groups put great faith in the power of the public schools. Properly run schools would "Americanize" immigrant children. The societies supported Bible reading in the public schools and opposed all aid to parochial schools. In the 1890s the Junior O.U.A.M. successfully sponsored a state law which required an American flag in every school. Here was a symbol for the children of foreign-born parents to revere. As the new immigration grew, so too did the patriotic orders. By 1915 the Junior O.U.A.M. claimed sixty-five thousand members in New Jersey. Jersey City alone had fifteen councils and five thousand members.

Impact of World War I

Nativism came to a head after 1914, when World War I began in Europe. Immigrants tended to support their home countries. The Irish and Germans opposed President Woodrow Wilson's pro-British policies. After the United States entered the war in 1917, German-Americans were treated as potential spies and saboteurs. Schools dropped German-language instruction, orchestras stopped performing Beethoven and Brahms, and restaurants renamed German dishes. Individual Germans were subjected to harassment and persecution by their non-German neighbors.

Anti-German hysteria during the war set the stage for anti-radical hysteria immediately thereafter. In 1919 and 1920 the federal government rounded up aliens suspected of radical politics and deported as many as it could. There were five hundred arrests in New Jersey alone. The raids in most cases amounted to gross violations of civil liberties and were later condemned. But they illustrate how popular feeling had turned against a free and open immigration policy. The 1920s would mark the beginning of a new era.

CHAPTER FOUR

Interlude, 1920–1960

When World War I ended in 1918, immigration to the United States soon resumed its prewar character. By early 1921 the Ellis Island processing center in New York harbor was so clogged with arriving immigrants that ships were diverted to other ports. But the balance of opinion had shifted against open entry. In May the first law limiting European immigration took effect.

Restriction and Quotas

The 1921 legislation set annual quotas for every European country. As one purpose of the act was to curtail immigration from southern and eastern Europe, these countries received only 15 percent of the allocation. Enacted hastily as temporary legislation, the 1921 law was overhauled in 1924 and 1927. The first revision made the quota system permanent. The second reduced total European immigration to 150,000 a year, not much more than 10 percent of peak prewar annual arrivals.

Quotas were based on the number of people in the United States who were descended from each European nationality. Thus new immigrants were to be admitted in a rough ratio with those already here. The discriminatory intent of restriction is well illustrated by one provision of the 1924 law. To establish quotas it used population figures for 1890, before most southern and eastern Europeans had entered the country. This further reduced immigration from those nations. Less harsh, the 1927 law based its calculations on the more recent 1920 census.

49

Although the national-origins quota system remained the core of immigration policy until 1965, it applied only to Europeans. Asians were treated separately. Congress had banned Chinese immigration since 1882 and by 1924 had excluded all Asians. Only North and South Americans were unaffected by restriction. They were able to immigrate freely until 1965.

Restriction resulted from native-born Protestants' fear that they would soon be overwhelmed in their own land. They saw themselves as fighting to preserve an embattled Anglo-Saxon tradition. They believed that immigrant groups that did not partake of that tradition threatened established American institutions. Native-born Protestants had lost their earlier confidence in their ability to make "Americans" of all who entered. Southern and eastern Europeans, they believed, could not be assimilated. Always uneasy with diversity, the native-born determined to reassert their authority. Their demands were reflected in the quota system. Under the 1927 law, 54 percent of the places went to Great Britain and Ireland. Italy and Poland received about 4 percent each. The quota system wrote into law the views of old-stock Americans as to which immigrants were desirable and which were not.

Restriction and quotas would have almost eliminated immigrants as a factor in the nation's population within a generation. But world events intervened. The disruptions and upheavals accompanying and following World War II forced changes in policy. Beginning in 1948 various classes of refugees and displaced persons were admitted outside the quota system. In spite of these exceptions, however, immigration never returned to its pre-1921 levels. The structure of restriction remained largely in place.

Those Who Returned

Today we tend to think of immigration as a one-way journey past "the lady with the lamp." Yet for many the experience was more complex. At least a third of those who entered between 1900 and 1920 eventually departed. Some had come to work hard and save money for a farm or small business at home. They accomplished their goals and returned home successful. Others never found a way to make a satisfactory living and returned without success. Still others just got homesick for familiar faces and familiar ways.

Of those who left, a significant number came back a second time. The decision to emigrate or return may have been intended as final, but changed circumstances altered lives and sent many people down new migratory paths. Sometimes immigration became a kind of seasonal migration, especially for unmarried males. Each fall, for example, before restriction changed the rules, a number of Italian laborers would return to Italy for the winter. They left when outdoor construction projects shut down, intending to return in the spring. Immigration, then, was very much an ebb and flow. Immigrant steamers did not return to Europe with empty decks.

Examples abound. Adamo Cerbone was born in Naples, Italy, in 1886. In 1903, at age seventeen, he emigrated to Bayonne. After a few years he returned to Italy and served three years in the Italian army. Back in Bayonne by 1911, he married, opened a grocery, and raised five children.

William Shaw and his wife left England for New York in the early 1880s. He worked as a harbor pilot, and they had at least two children. He then moved to Bombay, India, where he again worked as a harbor pilot. Eventually he returned to England to raise his growing family. In 1906 his son Vincent, who had been born in New York, returned to America as an immigrant. Vincent had been trained as a plumber. Like many immigrants he established himself in his trade, returned home briefly to marry, brought his wife back to New York, and settled down to raise a family.

But the story does not end there. In 1928 Vincent died of tuberculosis. His widow then made a prudent decision. She returned to England where she and her children would have the support of family. Her decision was meant to be final. But things did not work out as well as expected, and in less than two years she made another "final" decision. She brought her family back to New York City and eventually settled in suburban Essex County. Thus for the Shaw family the immigration experience involved three crossings and almost half a century.

Aging Immigrant Communities

With fewer new arrivals after restriction, the country's immigrant communities began to age and grow smaller. In 1920 the median age of immigrants was forty. That rose to fifty-one in 1940 and fifty-seven in 1960. In New Jersey the median age was fifty-eight in 1960, and for some groups it was even higher. For Italians the median was sixty-one; for Poles and Russians, sixty-two. The typical immigrant in 1960, then, was close to retirement. After 1930 the state's immigrant population began a steady decline, from a peak of 844,000 in that year to 615,000 in 1960. Indeed, in 1960 there were more immigrants in New Jersey over seventy-five than under twenty-five. Nature seemed ready to solve "the immigrant problem" in its own determined way.

Supporters of immigration restriction had anticipated this result. They also expected the end of free entry to lead to the rapid decline of ethnic cultures. They used the image of America as a "melting pot," a bubbling vat in which people of different cultural "flavors" would soon become blended into one. The finished brew, they confidently expected, would closely resemble old-stock America. The cultural attributes of the immigrants would quietly dissolve and finally disappear.

Enduring Ethnic Cultures

However, the critics of ethnicity did not consider the ability of the immigrants to transmit important elements of their cultures to their children. Ethnicity persisted and endured beyond the lives of the immigrants themselves. Those who grew up in immigrant households had their values and outlooks in large part shaped by family and neighborhood. What they learned there mattered to them for the rest of their lives, and it influenced how they in turn raised their children. The melting pot, then, did not quickly produce a smooth-textured broth. Instead, it produced something more akin to a lumpy stew.

Thus New Jersey retained much of its ethnic flavor. While most of its citizens were born in the United States, large numbers of these were molded by their immigrant heritage. In 1930 35 percent of New Jersey's residents had immigrant parents. After 1930 this figure started to decline as a third generation began to take the place of the second. But it did not decline rapidly. In 1960 a full 25 percent of New Jersey's population still consisted of second-generation ethnics. At least an equal number were third generation, the grandchildren of immigrants.

New Jersey provided a supportive environment for ethnic communities. Members of the second generation settled near their parents in the state's industrial cities. These ethnic clusters provided the population base necessary for maintaining various ethnic organizations, such as churches, clubs, and benefit societies. Religious institutions were the most important. Most of the "new" immigrants were Catholic or Jewish, which by itself set them apart from the older culture of Protestant America. Churches and synagogues became primary places for reenforcing ethnic identities and extending them across generational lines.

The small Lithuanian community in Paterson provides an example. After numerous petitions, the Catholic Church granted Paterson's Lithuanians a nationality parish in 1911. Members built a small wooden church within a year, and the parish prospered and endured. Although in 1962 there were fewer than eleven hundred Lithuanians in Paterson, the parish found the means to build a more substantial structure. Such nationality parishes provided a place for religious observances that incorporated appropriate national customs, ceremonies, and language.

Secular institutions served similar functions. Czechs and Slovaks brought the Sokol movement with them from central Europe. Sokol stressed physical fitness and cultural awareness and embodied Czech and Slovak nationalist aspirations. In America Sokol also served to promote the preservation of ethnic culture. Sokols were active in many New Jersey cities. Two of their summer camps in rural Morris County taught Slovak traditions to children of Slovak descent. Through Sokol, awareness of a shared heritage passed from one generation to the next.

Ethnicity and religion also shaped families. Together they worked to define the pool of acceptable marriage partners. Individuals living in large ethnic clusters tended to marry within the group, and their marriages reenforced concepts of ethnic identity and slowed the drift toward assimilation. For the immigrant generation and its children, marriage outside the nationality group was rare. But intermarriage rates increased with each

These children are in Latvian dress. Parents tried to instill a sense of ethnic identity and pride in their children. From the LIDUMS FAMILY COLLECTION, courtesy BALCH INSTITUTE FOR ETHNIC STUDIES.

generation as ethnic identities grew weaker. Even then, people who married outside their own ethnic group still tended to marry within the same religion. The divorce rate has also been influenced by ethnicity and religion. Catholics generally have divorced less frequently than the American average. Italian Catholics, who place great importance on family solidarity, have always had one of the lowest divorce rates in the country.

Ethnic Politics

Ethnic issues continued to shape the state's political life, although immigrants and ethnics never constituted a unified interest group. The differences between immigrant groups were too great to allow a general sense of collective identity, and immigrant groups themselves frequently lacked internal unity. Italians, for example, were divided by regional loyalties and attachments which made collective action all but impossible. They thought of themselves as Neopolitan or Piedmontese or

Sicilian. Consequently their political influence was comparatively weak. Only the second generation, reared in America, had a clear sense of themselves as "Italians." They tended to be more successful in creating an Italian presence in New Jersey politics.

Ethnic politics reached its height in Jersey City. Frank Hague put together a political organization that controlled the city from 1920 to 1947. Jersey City's Irish provided the base of support, but the organization reached out to provide patronage and minor offices to members of other ethnic groups. The organization consolidated its power by creating a coalition of ethnic blocs led by the Irish. While Mayor Hague's administration was corrupt in many ways, it was responsive to the cultural values of its constituents. Hague enforced a morality acceptable to working-class Catholics. Drinking and petty gambling were tolerated, but more serious vices like prostitution and narcotics were eliminated quickly.

The "Continental" morality was challenged by Prohibition. As described earlier, decades of native Protestants had objected to immigrant attitudes toward the use of alcohol. Prohibition marked the culmination of their long struggle to control immigrant and ethnic behavior by eliminating access to liquor. In New Jersey it pitted native "drys" against ethnic "wets."

Taking effect in 1920, Prohibition was unpopular in New Jersey's ethnic communities. No city administration could support strict enforcement and survive at the polls. Liquor was easy to find in most cities. In Newark a brewery sold the ingredients for homemade beer, and the public library reported that patrons had torn the instructions for wine making out of its recipe books. When repeal took effect in 1933, a street party at one reopened Newark brewery lasted two days.

Old-fashioned nativism returned to New Jersey for another visit in the 1920s. For several years the Ku Klux Klan gained in popularity among native Protestants. The Klan appealed to those who supported immigration restriction, feared Catholic influence, or opposed the way ethnic communities ignored Prohibition. Suburban towns close to large cities, such as Bloomfield and Montclair, provided much support. In Newark, two thousand residents joined George Washington Klan #3. Although the Klan was dying by 1930, its presence in New Jersey illustrates the persistence of ethnic and religious conflict.

Weakening Ethnic Ties

In spite of the strength of ethnic cultures, there were forces at work that gradually wore them down. If an ethnic minority is to endure for generations it must preserve its language. This proved difficult in New Jersey's cities. Work, school, and leisure brought the members of ethnic groups into contact with outsiders. The large number of immigrant languages compounded the problem. Immigrants needed to communicate with each other as well as with native-born Americans. Consequently, most learned at least some English, and nearly all their children spoke it well. By the third generation the original language was generally lost, and with it went a vital piece of ethnic identification.

Economic success itself worked to weaken ethnic ties. Immigrants who prospered usually had regular contact with the larger society and tended to move closer to the American mainstream. Often they became leaders in the ethnic community, serving as organization officers and as spokesmen in ward and city politics. A good example is Polish immigrant Anthony Dworzanski of Bayonne. A leader in the 1916 Standard Oil strike, he next founded a Polish mutual aid society. Later he joined the Bayonne police force, rising to lieutenant. Eventually he became Bayonne's commissioner of public works. Successful immigrants like Dworzanksi acted as role models and mediators, aiding the accommodation of immigrants to American ways.

The relationship between economic success and assimilation showed up in a 1939 survey of radio listening habits. The survey found that almost all of Newark's Italian immigrants listened to New York City's Italian-language radio stations. But only half of the second generation listened, and their listening was related to income. The more money people earned, the less likely they were to prefer Italian-language programming. That those who succeeded economically preferred English-language radio indicates their greater degree of assimilation.

After World War II New Jersey's ethnics joined the migration to the suburbs. They left the old urban neighborhoods for places like Westfield, Cherry Hill, and Cedar Grove. Suburbs blended people more completely into American mass culture. Social class and religion were the organizing themes of suburbia, and ethnic traditions were often discarded. Catholics who left the nationality parishes of the cities joined the territorial parishes of the suburbs. Territorial parishes included all Catholics in a community. Irish, Polish, and Italian ethnics worshipped and socialized together as Catholics rather than as members of nationality groups.

A study of Jews in suburban Essex County in the 1950s found similar processes at work. Jews who moved to the suburbs did not take the secular institutions of the Jewish neighborhoods with them. In their place, the synagogue assumed a new importance. Only 40 percent of suburban Jews had been synagogue members before moving. But almost 80 percent joined in the suburbs. Thus the religious rather than the secular dimensions of Jewish ethnicity were adapted to the suburbs. The ethnic differences among the descendants of German, Polish, and Russian Jews diminished in suburbia.

With language discarded, traditions only half remembered, and migration to the suburbs emptying the old neighborhoods, New Jersey's ethnic cultures were drifting slowly toward oblivion by 1960. Religion proved to be the most enduring ethnic inheritance. Increasingly people identified themselves primarily as Protestant, Catholic, or Jewish. The immigrant and ethnic paths by which they had gotten there mattered less and less. They were Protestant, Catholic, or Jewish Americans. And that was enough.

CHAPTER FIVE

The Third Wave, 1960–

By 1960 the era of immigration and strong ethnic identities appeared to be coming to a close. But changes were already under way that would soon bring large numbers of Hispanics and Asians into the United States, adding new elements to American ethnicity. Large numbers of immigrants once again began to pass through New York City entry points. As in the past, many chose to settle in New Jersey.

Puerto Ricans

The first Hispanics to arrive in large numbers were Puerto Ricans. Since the United States had acquired Puerto Rico from Spain in 1898 and granted its residents citizenship in 1917, Puerto Ricans are actually migrants rather than immigrants. Therefore their movement to the mainland is not controlled by the barriers erected to limit immigration. Nevertheless, their roots in the Spanish-speaking culture of the Caribbean mark them as a distinct ethnic group in American society.

In many respects Puerto Rican migration resembled earlier European immigration. Puerto Rico underwent an economic upheaval after World War II that disrupted its traditional agricultural society. Disruption set people adrift, and these were the people most likely to become migrants, willing to seek work and a more secure life outside of Puerto Rico. Those who left for the mainland tended to be better educated, more skilled, and more familiar with urban life than those who stayed behind.

Migration out of Puerto Rico centered on New York City.

Once pioneers had established small communities, it was easy for others to join. People came to link up with relatives and friends, establishing chains of migration. Old migrants helped recent arrivals adapt to life in a strange and often hostile environment. Between 1950 and 1980 New York City's Puerto Rican population grew from 254,000 to 860,000. By 1960 the city's two long-time Italian-language radio stations had both switched to Spanish. This, wrote the *New York Times*, "reflects the growth of the city's Spanish-speaking population as well as they decline in the numbers of older immigrant groups."[1]

New Jersey's Puerto Rican population grew as an extension of migration to New York City. Between 1950 and 1980 the number of Puerto Ricans in New Jersey rose from under ten thousand to more than 240,000. Like the Europeans who preceded them, most settled in the industrial centers near New York City. In 1980 57 percent lived in Hudson, Essex, and Passaic counties. Puerto Ricans frequently occupied the older neighborhoods that more established ethnic groups had discarded in favor of the suburbs.

Puerto Ricans entered a changing economy. When European immigration was at its height in the early twentieth century, basic manufacturing was expanding rapidly and required increasing numbers of unskilled factory workers. After 1950, however, the expanding areas of the economy demanded workers with technical or professional skills. Manufacturing began to decline and people without skills or education had more and more difficulty finding work.

The newcomers were not well prepared for this. In 1970 New Jersey's Puerto Rican migrants averaged 8.1 years of education. Only 10 percent had completed high school. As a result, they generally held low-paying jobs and often were unemployed. Twenty-seven percent of Puerto Rican families lived below the official poverty line. Average household income was lower than that of any other New Jersey ethnic group.

Puerto Rican leaders claimed that one cause of Puerto Rican economic distress was the ease with which migrants could return home. Many who came to the mainland, they noted, saw themselves as only temporary residents and therefore lacked the commitment needed to succeed in a new environment. And many Puerto Ricans did return, even more than earlier European immigrants. In one year, while 10,600 children transferred to New York City schools from Puerto Rico, sixty-five hundred transferred the other way.

In the 1970s Puerto Ricans in New Jersey began to create and support organizations which they hoped would lead to political and economic gains. A two-day confrontation between Puerto Ricans and police in Newark in 1974 forced that city to look more closely at the frustrations and grievances of its Puerto Rican population. The Newark Human Rights Commission identified discrimination in public and private employment as a major factor in Puerto Rican unemployment and poverty. Although the commission urged a number of reforms, little changed. The percentage of Puerto Rican households living below the government's official poverty line actually increased from 27 percent in 1970 to 37.5 percent in 1980.

Native Blacks

One of the largest migrations in American history was that of native blacks from the rural South to the cities of the North. Black migration had many parallels with its Puerto Rican counterpart. Between 1940 and 1990, New Jersey's black population grew from 190,000 to 980,000. The largest black communities were in and around Newark. Because of its size and importance, New Jersey's black population is treated in another book published by the Historical Commission, *Afro-Americans in New Jersey: A Short History,* by Giles R. Wright.

Immigration Law

The restrictions Congress enacted in the 1920s to control immigration were based on racist assumptions about the undesirability of certain types of people. After World War II these assumptions became increasingly hard to justify and came under frequent criticism. In 1965 Congress rewrote immigration law, abandoning the national-origins quota system with its bias against southern and eastern Europeans and its virtual exclusion of Asians.

The new law established an annual quota of 290,000 immigrants, 170,000 from the Eastern Hemisphere and 120,000 from the Western. No more than twenty thousand could come from any single country. For the first time numerical restrictions applied to immigration from North and South America. The new law gave first preference to people who had relatives already living in the United States. Up to 74 percent of the annual quota could be used to reunite families. After that, preference went first to people with needed job skills and then to refugees.

While the new policy was free of overt racial and ethnic bias, those who supported it did not expect much change in the sources of immigration. After all, they reasoned, it was Europeans—and only Europeans—who already had relatives here or who possessed the kinds of skills required to qualify under the job preference categories. Few Latin Americans had chosen to immigrate even when no restrictions applied to them, and officials believed that there were not enough Asians in the country for the family preference categories to matter much. Thus the new policy was expected to favor Europeans even though it did not specifically label them as more desirable.

But policymakers could not foresee the political and economic upheavals in Latin America that would lead to large-scale emigration. Nor did they take into account the fact that immigration has always proceeded through kin-based migration chains, and that over time these chains can move large numbers of people. A married Korean or Colombian male entering with a needed skill, for example, can immediately bring in his wife and children. Once citizens, husband and wife can both sponsor parents, brothers, and sisters. They, in turn, can bring in their kin.

And immigrants have done exactly that. Through kin-based migration chains, immigration from Latin America and Asia has grown year by year. An immigration official described a typical naturalization ceremony in 1977: "We swore in about seven hundred people. They became new citizens at noon, and by one o'clock our office . . . was jammed with the same people who were now petitioning for other members of their families to come to the United States."[2]

At the same time, immigration from Europe started to decline. After 1960 western European economies began to provide sufficient prosperity to keep most likely emigrants at home. In Communist eastern Europe, where living standards were much lower, government policies generally discouraged emigration. By 1980 Europeans were a distinct minority of those entering the United States as immigrants.

Illegal Immigrants

Entering the country through the preference system is one way to immigrate. Another is to cross the border without documents or with false documents. Such entry is illegal, and those who are caught face deportation. For those who do not qualify under the law as immigrants or refugees, however, the benefits are often seen as worth the risks. People from very poor countries, such as Haiti or Mexico, may feel they have little to lose. The 1980 census estimated the number of illegal—or undocumented—aliens at three to five million, or as much as 2 percent of the nation's population. Illegal immigrants mix easily in communities of legal immigrants, and New Jersey certainly has its share. A 1975 estimate put the figure at three hundred thousand, a little over 4 percent of the state's residents. In one sweep of undocumented workers in Newark, two were found employed as guards at the local FBI office.

Two sociologists studied the means by which a large Dominican family left the Dominican Republic and reconstituted itself in the United States. Family members entered legally whenever possible. Where legal entry was not possible, or would take a long time, the family went around the law. Members used such devices as claiming false relationships with one another to qualify for admittance under the kinship categories, traveling on rented passports, and entering into short-term marriages with citizens of the United States ("matrimonio de favor") to gain citizenship.

Illegal immigration is a complex problem with no easy solution. In 1986 Congress enacted amnesty legislation which made it possible for illegal immigrants who had been in the country continuously since 1981 to become legal residents. The new law also made employers responsible for checking the legal status of the workers they hire. But these changes were not expected to have a major impact on the number of people willing to enter the country without documents. To date, only a small percentage of the estimated total number of illegal aliens has applied for amnesty. Illegal immigration remains one of the major unresolved issues of our time.

Impact on New Jersey

Immigration from Latin America and Asia is having a major impact on New Jersey. Relatively few immigrants now come from Europe. Table 4 compares two groups of immigrants living in New Jersey in 1980: those who arrived in the 1950s, and those who entered between 1975 and 1980. The countries of origin for those who came in the 1950s looks very similar to the countries of origin listed in Table 3 (page 38) for immigrants in New Jersey in 1920. The places from which immigrants came did not change much in fifty years; however, between 1960 and 1975 a major change took place. By the late 1970s most immigrants were Latin American or Asian. Only three European countries—Italy, Poland, and Great Britain—appear in both of Table 4's columns.

A disproportionate number of immigrants to the United States today choose to locate in New Jersey. While the state has about 3 percent of the nation's population, it routinely attracts close to 6 percent of new immigrants. In 1984 only four states—California, New York, Texas, and Florida—attracted more immigrants than the 27,148 drawn to New Jersey.

Recent immigration has reversed an important population trend. New Jersey's foreign-born population gradually fell from a peak of 26 percent in 1910 to 8.5 percent in 1970. Between 1970 and 1980, however, it rose to 10.3 percent. As long as present immigration patterns persist—and they show no signs of changing soon—the percentage of New Jersey's people who are immigrants or the children of immigrants will continue to grow. New Jersey is once again becoming an immigrant state.

Like their predecessors, recent immigrants are not evenly distributed across the state. Most live in urbanized northeastern New Jersey, close to New York City. In 1980 half of those who immigrated between 1970 and 1980 lived in Hudson, Essex, and Passaic counties, and nearly one-quarter lived in adjacent Bergen and Union counties. In the same year about one-fourth of the population of Hudson County was foreign-born and 39 percent spoke a language other than English in the home. In the five northeastern counties more than seven hundred thousand people—22 percent of the population—did not use English at home. The number has undoubtedly increased since 1980.

Table 4

Place of Origin of Persons in New Jersey in 1980 Who Immigrated during Two Periods

	Immigrated 1950–1959			Immigrated 1975–1980	
Place	Number	Percentage	Place	Number	Percentage
1. Germany	18,338	16.7	1. India	8,307	6.8
2. Italy	17,724	16.1	2. Portugal	7,520	6.1
3. Poland	7,967	7.2	3. Colombia	6,577	5.4
4. Great Britain	7,009	6.4	4. Philippines	6,323	5.2
5. U.S.S.R.	5,885	5.4	5. Dominican Republic	5,469	4.5
6. Hungary	5,347	4.9	6. Korea	4,780	3.9
7. Cuba	5,002	4.5	7. Japan	3,928	3.2
8. Ireland*	3,744	3.4	8. Great Britain	3,865	3.2
9. Canada	2,731	2.5	9. Italy	3,746	3.1
10. Netherlands	2,514	2.3	10. Cuba	3,682	3.0
11. Yugoslavia	2,402	2.2	11. Jamaica	3,551	2.9
12. Greece	2,306	2.1	12. Poland	2,888	2.3
Other	28,883	26.3	Other	61,563	50.4
TOTAL	109,852	100.0	TOTAL	122,199	100.0

*Includes Northern and Southern Ireland.

SOURCE: United States Census, 1880, New Jersey, Table 195.

Cubans

After Puerto Ricans, Cubans are the largest Hispanic group in New Jersey. Between 1950 and 1960 the number of Cubans in the state grew from under one thousand to about fifty-five hundred. During the 1960s the political and economic upheavals that followed Fidel Castro's successful Cuban revolution led to the forced or voluntary departure of several hundred thousand. Most came to the the United States, admitted as refugees; others went to Spain or South America. By 1970 fifty-nine thousand Cubans lived in New Jersey. By 1980 the number had grown to sixty-eight thousand.

In contrast to Puerto Ricans, most of those who left Cuba were well educated and highly skilled. Many had professional or business backgrounds. After an often difficult adjustment to a new environment, Cubans have achieved a fair degree of economic success. The 1980 census showed them to be the most prosperous Hispanic group in New Jersey.

Although immigrants tend to cluster together whenever possible, Cubans have done so to an extraordinary degree. In 1980 57 percent lived in Hudson County alone, and 91 percent lived in the five northeastern urban counties. More than 40 percent lived in just two crowded cities: West New York and Union City, located north of Hoboken along the Hudson River. More than thirty-three thousand Cubans reside in these two towns. The Cuban presence has attracted other Spanish-speaking peoples. In 1980 Union City's population was 32 percent Cuban, 32 percent other Hispanic, and 36 percent non-Hispanic; in 1990 the city was 76 percent Hispanic. In these Spanish-speaking communities even Asian restaurants print their menus in Spanish.

Cubans place a high value on strong family ties, and these ties have helped sustain immigration. A study of West New York Cubans in the 1970s found that nearly all had known someone in the United States before emigrating, usually a family member. Established immigrants helped new arrivals find housing and jobs and adjust to American ways. Cubans had problems with English and with other aspects of American society. The greater independence given children in American households became a particular source of tension within Cuban families.

Most Cubans who arrived as refugees after 1960 did not think of themselves as true immigrants. They saw themselves instead as temporary exiles who would return to Cuba after Castro's downfall. They were not interested in surrendering their Cuban identity, and many supported anti-Castro political organizations. But as time passed and Castro endured, they became increasingly involved, sometimes in spite of themselves, in the society that surrounded them. And they watched uncomfortably as their children grew up more American than Cuban.

The Cubans who adapted most easily to the United States were educated people who spoke English well and were financially successful. As with Italians half a century before, successful Cubans showed a greater preference for English-language newspapers, radio, and television. Those less well versed in English or less prosperous remained more completely enmeshed in Hispanic culture. But gradually New Jersey came to feel like home to many Cubans. As one Union City woman told a newspaper reporter, "Even if Castro left Cuba today, I could never go back now. I'm American. I can't even eat Cuban food anymore."[3]

Other Hispanics and West Indians

About 20 percent of New Jersey's Hispanics are neither Puerto Rican nor Cuban. These people come from almost every country in Latin America and the Caribbean Islands. Some countries are more heavily represented than others. Few Mexicans or Central Americans have found their way to New Jersey. They have settled in the West and Southwest. Although Mexicans make up 60 percent of all Hispanics nationally, they account for less than 3 percent of Hispanics in New Jersey.

After Puerto Ricans and Cubans, the state's two largest Hispanic groups in 1980 were Colombians (twenty thousand) and Dominicans (fourteen thousand). As with Hispanics generally, they were concentrated (83 percent) in the five northeastern urban counties, and four counties—Cape May, Gloucester, Salem, and Warren—contained no Dominicans at all. Colombians and Dominicans sought freedom from political and social turmoil as well as economic opportunity. Although most were reasonably well educated, they frequently were unable to find work appropriate to their skills. Dominicans typically find work in restaurants, hotels, and the garment industry. A large percentage of both Colombians and Dominicans eventually return home.

Two West Indian groups in New Jersey are not Hispanic. Jamaicans are English-speaking; Haitians are French-speaking. Both are predominantly black and have settled primarily in Essex and Passaic counties. Jamaicans, often well educated, frequently open neighborhood shops or other small businesses. Haitians, on the other hand, come from the poorest country in the Western Hemisphere. In recent years boatloads have fled Haiti's violence, repression, and desperate poverty. They have sought entry, often without success, as political refugees. Lacking skills and often poorly educated, Haitians have had great difficulty establishing a foothold in New Jersey's economy.

Asians

Immigration from Asia has grown steadily since 1965. While most Asians settle in the states along the Pacific coast, New York and New Jersey have become secondary settlement areas. Between 1960 and 1980 New Jersey's Asian-born population grew from fifteen thousand to ninety-six thousand, and in 1990 272,000 New Jersey residents claimed Asian birth or ancestry. The majority of Asian immigrants came from eastern Asia, including India, China, and Japan. The three largest Asian groups in New Jersey in 1980 were Indians (19,500), Filipinos (18,200), and Koreans (10,700). Not all Asian immigrants to the United States are equally drawn to New Jersey.

While the state regularly attracts about 10 percent of all Indians, it draws a scant 1 percent of Southeast Asians, such as Vietnamese and Laotians.

Asians who come to New Jersey arrive with a number of advantages. First, most are very well educated. Among adults who arrived in the 1970s, more than half had at least four years of college, and almost a third had additional graduate training. Among Indians and Filipinos, two-thirds had college degrees and two-fifths had some education beyond college. The average Asian immigrant has more education than the average native-born American.

Moreover, the majority of Asians, unlike most Hispanics, arrive with a good command of English. Among Asians who arrived in the 1970s, only 4 percent did not speak any English, while 80 percent were fully fluent. (Almost 90 percent of Indians and 95 percent of Filipinos arrived with a good or excellent command of the language.)

Consequently, Asians are frequently found in relatively high-status jobs. In 1980 two-fifths of employed Asian immigrants in New Jersey were classified as managers and professionals, compared to a quarter of the state's work force generally. As a result, Asian families had the highest average incomes of any group in New Jersey, immigrant or native. Filipinos and Indians—the best educated and most fluent in English—comprise the largest proportion of managers and professionals among all Asians. Members of both groups are frequently found in the medical professions, especially in full-time hospital work. About 10 percent of all the doctors practicing anesthesiology in the country today are Indian. Not surprisingly, in 1980 Filipinos and Indians had the highest family incomes of all ethnic groups in New Jersey, including native whites.

Like other immigrants, most Asians have concentrated in northeastern New Jersey. Above average incomes, however, have led them to settle more in the suburbs than in the old central cities. In 1990 more of the state's Asians lived in suburban Bergen, Middlesex, and Morris counties (43 percent) than in the traditional immigrant centers of Hudson, Essex, and Passaic (26 percent). Even within the urban counties they tend not to settle in central cities. For example, in 1990 15 percent of Essex County's Asians lived in Newark, as compared to 73 percent of Hispanics. In the Trenton area, only 6 percent of Mercer County's Asians lived in Trenton itself, compared to 63 percent of its Hispanics.

Although traditional immigrant neighborhoods are hard to establish in the suburbs, Asians have tended to locate more in some communities than others. Clifton in the Paterson-Passaic area, Cherry Hill outside of Camden, and Edison near New Brunswick are all examples of suburban towns with relatively large concentrations of Asians.

No Asian nationality has clustered to the extent of the state's small but growing Japanese population. Of the ninety-nine hundred Japanese in New Jersey in 1980, almost half lived in

Bergen County and two thousand of them lived in the small Hudson River community of Fort Lee. In 1980 they were Fort Lee's third largest ethnic group, after Italians and Russians. Most were recent immigrants. Living close to other Japanese provided the security of the familiar in the midst of a new and different environment.

Not all Asians are affluent or suburban. In 1980 6.1 percent of Asian families lived below the poverty line, compared to a state average of 7.5 percent. For these Asians, adjustment to the United States was more difficult, and they were more likely to live in central cities. Jersey City housed the state's largest Asian population. Eight thousand Asians, 60 percent of whom were Filipinos, lived in the state's most immigrant major city.

Like their European predecessors, some Asians have turned to small shops and businesses as avenues to modest prosperity. Especially attractive are niches in the economy which can be entered with little capital and in which success is achieved through long hours, hard work, and the labor of several family members. In the New York City area Koreans operate over one thousand fresh fruit and vegetable stores. Often they buy out elderly Jewish or Italian immigrants who want to retire. Indians operate about 70 percent of New York City's newsstands and more than a quarter of the nation's non-chain motels. These are all examples of labor-intensive businesses with relatively low start-up costs. They are also businesses to which several family members, including adolescent children, can contribute.

Immigrants frequently help each other get established and do business within the group whenever possible. New Jersey life insurance agent Jaydev Patel of Livingston is a good example. He is his company's most successful agent, with four thousand clients across the country. Almost all of them are other Indian immigrants.

Portuguese

Between 1960 and 1980 the number of European immigrants in New Jersey declined as deaths exceeded new arrivals. Portugal was the one conspicuous exception. Portuguese immigration to the United States increased sharply after 1965. Between 1960 and 1980 New Jersey's Portuguese population grew from four thousand to twenty-eight thousand. Almost 75 percent settled in and around Newark and Elizabeth, joining small Portuguese communities established in the 1920s. Here they built the churches and clubs of a closely knit ethnic community. In Newark the Sport Club Portugus owned a large facility and in 1980 claimed more than one thousand members. Arriving with little education and poor command of English, the Portuguese found work primarily as factory operatives and unskilled laborers. In 1980 less than 4 percent were in professional or managerial occupations.

Suburban Ethnics

As Hispanics, other immigrants, and native blacks moved into the old urban areas, the descendants of earlier European immigrants continued their trek to the suburbs. A descendant of Greek immigrants told a reporter that before 1950, "we were all clannish and crowded together around the [Greek Orthodox] church. . . . Now it is different. Almost everybody has it made and moves out to the suburbs."[4]

In 1980 Bergen County led the state in the number of American-born residents of Irish, German, Italian, and Greek ancestry. Middlesex led in Poles and Hungarians. Both counties were home to significant numbers of Asians; neither contained many blacks or Hispanics.* Only those recent immigrants who arrived with skills that allowed them to buy into a middle-class life style soon after arrival were well represented in suburbia; other immigrants, by far the majority, lived in the same neighborhoods—and often in the same well-worn buildings—as had the immigrant ancestors of today's suburban ethnics.

Whether or not the children and grandchildren of today's immigrants will eventually join the descendants of earlier arrivals in the suburbs remains to be seen. And if they do, who will take their places in the inner cities?

---

*Two older Middlesex County cities are exceptions. New Brunswick was almost 30 percent black and Perth Amboy 40 percent Hispanic in 1980. These are examples of "central cities" in predominantly suburban counties.

Interest in ethnicity remains strong, as this performance by the Bayern Verein German Dance Group at the Garden State Arts Center illustrates. Photograph by HARVEY BILKER, NEWARK STAR LEDGER, courtesy NEW JERSEY NEWS PHOTOS.

CONCLUSION

For most of the 350 years since the Dutch settled Bergen, New Jersey has been home to large numbers of immigrants. Only twice has the rushing stream of new arrivals dwindled to a trickle. The first period was in the decades between the Revolution and 1840. The second was in the years after immigration restriction began in the 1920s.

Since colonial times, New Jersey's population has contained more immigrants and more ethnic diversity than most of the nation. As we have seen, this has been both a stimulus to economic and urban growth and the source of some rather serious conflicts.

Since the middle of the nineteenth century, Americans have debated the worth of immigration. On the one hand, they have celebrated the "open door" and the diversity of a pluralistic society. It is with good reason that "the lady with the lamp" remains one of our more powerful national symbols. On the other hand, that same pluralism has seemed rather threatening when immigrant communities have challenged the positions and perspectives of dominant interests. Then Americans talk about the need for "assimilation" and about looking more closely at just who enters through that open door.

Economic Impact

One recurring issue has been the economic impact of immigrants on American society. Some labor leaders and others have charged that immigrants take work away from Americans and lower wage rates by increasing the competition for available jobs. They have used this argument to justify restricting immigration. Yet immigrants also create jobs. They are consumers and must be housed, clothed, and fed. While immigrants certainly take jobs that might go to some Americans, they just as surely create opportunities for others.

In nineteenth-century New Jersey, immigration greatly quickened the pace of urbanization and industrialization and helped revive a generally stagnant economy. Among the slowest-growing states in the first half of the nineteenth century, New Jersey was one of the fastest-growing in the second half.

In recent years the state's growth has again come largely from immigration. Between 1970 and 1980 its population grew from 7.1 to 7.3 million people. All of that increase came from immigration and the continued migration of blacks and Puerto Ricans. The number of native-born whites of native-born parents fell by about 400,000. But for immigration and migration, New Jersey would have lost population during the 1970s. Certainly much of the growth in New Jersey's economy and the renewed vitality of some of its older cities must be credited to the state's continuing popularity with new arrivals.

Nativism Today

As we have seen, past immigrants did not always receive a warm welcome. Most recently both Asians and Hispanics have become the targets of discrimination and criticism. Asians have stirred resentment for their success in the American economy and in American schools and colleges. Almost 10 percent of the freshman class at Princeton in recent years has been of Asian origin, although Asians account for less than 2 percent of the country's population. Racially motivated violence against Asians, especially over competition for jobs, is a growing national problem.

Hispanics have also suffered discrimination. In New Jersey discrimination in hiring has long been recognized as a factor in Puerto Rican poverty. Non-Hispanics resent Hispanic competition. A descendant of German immigrants in Union City told a reporter, "You've got to be Spanish-speaking to get a job. The Cubans, they come over, they get everything. We Americans don't get nothing. The companies would rather have the Spanish working for them because they work for peanuts." Another was even more blunt: "Those Cubans—we should put them back on their boats and sink them. We don't have enough work for our own people."[1]

Language

Language has always been an important ethnic issue. Immigrants seek to maintain their native tongue, while older-stock Americans oppose recognizing any language other than English. The very diversity of immigrants in America has meant that no single language has competed with English, as does French in parts of Canada. While Hoboken and other cities met demands for German-language schools in the nineteenth century, this was the exception. Thus English was more easily preserved as the dominant tongue.

Language is a source of conflict again today, particularly in the field of education. At issue is how quickly schools should impose English on non-English-speaking children. In 1968 Congress mandated that children whose first language was not English receive some instruction in the language and culture of their parents. The law remains controversial. Older-stock Americans complain that it slows down assimilation, which they want schools to promote and encourage.

Immigrants in every era have worked to maintain their ethnic identity and pass significant aspects of it on to their children. Conflicts between immigrants and natives over language and culture are enduring, and will probably last as long as immigration and ethnicity matter in American life. The quest for harmony is more difficult in a pluralistic society.

A Pluralistic Future

Once again immigration is reshaping New Jersey. Between 1970 and 1980 the immigrant portion of the state's population increased to slightly more than 10 percent, the first increase since 1910. In the 1980s almost 25,000 new immigrants settled in New Jersey each year. Most were Asian and Latin American. Few Europeans emigrated, and the number of European immigrants in New Jersey continued to shrink year by year. In 1970 three-fourths of New Jersey's immigrants were Europeans. By 1980 that figure had declined to slightly more than half. In 1990 non-Europeans constituted a majority of the state's foreign-born. This marks a major divide in New Jersey history.

It is unlikely that immigration patterns will change soon. Nor are major changes in immigration law expected. New Jersey will

The Statue of Liberty, with Ellis Island in the background, captures the spirit of our immigrant past, present, and future. Courtesy NATIONAL PARK SERVICE, STATUE OF LIBERTY NATIONAL MONUMENT.

continue to attract significant numbers of documented and undocumented new arrivals. Its population will come increasingly from Asia, Latin America, and the Caribbean basin. As time passes, they too will attempt to shape New Jersey in their image, just as previous immigrants have tried to do. Tensions, conflicts, and a new accommodation will surely result.

However, if we believe that immigrants made the state and nation stronger in the past, then there is every reason to believe they will continue to do so in the present and future. Whatever the challenges and tensions that immigration may create, it still remains a major source of social and economic vitality. And that vitality, across the generations, has left its indelible mark on New Jersey and its people.

NOTES

Full citations are found in "Sources," p. 78.

Introduction

1. Glazer, *Ethnic Dilemmas, 1964–1982,* 234.

Chapter One

1. Leiby, *The Early Dutch and Swedish Settlers of New Jersey,* 30.

Chapter Two

1. McClure, "The Entering Wedge," 6.
2. David Bishop to E. B. Earl, A. D. Wilson and J. W. Smith, February 1853.
3. Deshler, "The Great American Middle Class," 17.
4. Newell, "Governor's Message," 21–22.
5. Jersey City *American Standard,* 21 June 1862.
6. New York *Irish American,* 23 November 1878.

Chapter Three

1. Howe, *World of Our Fathers,* 41.
2. Churchill, *The Italians of Newark,* 43.
3. Ibid., p. 61.
4. Vecoli, *People of New Jersey,* 182.
5. Schonbach, *Radicals and Visionaries,* 60.
6. Bukowczyk, "The Transformation of Working Class Ethnicity," 68.
7. "The Patriotic Order Sons of America: Something About the Order," 10–11.

Chapter Five

1. *New York Times,* 16 July 1959, p. 25, and 3 June 1960, p. 60.
2. Crewdson, *The Tarnished Door,* 117.
3. *Washington Post* 7 July 1980, p. 6, 15.
4. "State is Home to Hundreds of Cypriotes," *The New York Times,* 17 February 1975, p. 48.

Conclusion

1. *The Washington Post,* 7 July 1980, p. 15.

SOURCES

Introduction

Nathan Glazer, *Ethnic Dilemmas, 1964–1982* (Cambridge, Mass., 1983)
Brinley Thomas, *Migration and Economic Growth,* 2nd ed. (Cambridge, Mass., 1973)

Chapter One

Wesley Frank Craven, *New Jersey and the English Colonization of North America* (New York, 1964)
Adrian C. Leiby, *The Early Dutch and Swedish Settlers of New Jersey* (New York, 1964)
Richard P. McCormick, *New Jersey From Colony to State,* rev. ed. (Newark, 1981)
John E. Pomfret, *Colonial New Jersey: A History* (New York, 1973)
Thomas L. Purvis, "The European Origins of New Jersey's Eighteenth-Century Population," *New Jersey History* 100 (Spring/Summer 1982), 15–31
Statistical View of the United States (Washington, D.C., 1854)
Rudolph J. Vecoli, *The People of New Jersey* (Princeton, 1965)

Chapter Two

David Bishop to E. B. Karl, A. D. Wilson and J. W. Smith, February 1853, Bishop Papers, Rutgers University
John Bodnar, *The Transplanted: A History of Immigrants in Urban America* (Bloomington, Ind., 1985)
John T. Cunningham, *Newark* (Newark, 1966)
Charles D. Deshler, "The Great American Middle Class. An Address Delivered Before the Order of United Americans of Newark, N.J., February 22, 1855," (New York, 1855)
Jay P. Dolan, *The American Catholic Experience: A History From Colonial Times to the Present* (New York, 1985)
Joseph M. Flynn, *The Catholic Church in New Jersey* (Morristown, 1904)

Herbert G. Gutman, *Work, Culture and Society in Industrializing America* (New York, 1976)

Lawrence J. McCaffrey, *The Irish Diaspora in America* (Bloomington, Ind., 1976)

A. W. McClure, "The Entering Wedge," in *The School Question: A Correspondence Between Rev. J. Kelly of St. Peter's (R.C.) Church and Rev. A. W. McClure, of the First Reformed Dutch Church, Jersey City* (New York, 1853), 6–8

Manual of the Common Council of Jersey City (Jersey City, 1858)

William A. Newell, "Governor's Message," in *Appendix to the Minutes of the Eighty-Fourth General Assembly of the State of New Jersey,* (Freehold, 1860)

Raymond M. Ralph, "The City and the Church: Catholic Beginnings in Newark, 1840–1870," *New Jersey History* 96 (Autumn/Winter 1978): 105–18

William E. Sackett, *Modern Battles of Trenton* (Trenton, 1895), I

Douglas V. Shaw, *The Making of An Immigrant City: Ethnic and Cultural Conflict in Jersey City, New Jersey, 1850–1877* (New York, 1976)

Vecoli, *People of New Jersey*

Also these newspapers: *New York Tablet,* 19 September–14 November 1857; *Jersey City American Standard,* 19–26 June 1862; *Jersey City Evening Journal,* 9 October 1871; 16 June 1873; *New York Irish American,* 23 November 1878; and *Truth* (New York), 9 July 1882

And: Federal Manuscript Census Schedules of Jersey City, New Jersey, 1860, National Archives Microfilm Publication, Roll 653–693.

Chapter Three

Bodnar, *The Transplanted*

Joseph Brandes, *Immigrants to Freedom: Jewish Communities in Rural New Jersey Since 1882* (Philadelphia, 1971)

John W. Briggs, "Fertility and Cultural Change Among Families in Italy and America," *The American Historical Review* 91 (December 1986): 1129–45

John J. Bukowczyk, "The Transformation of Working Class Ethnicity: Corporate Control, Americanization, and the Polish Immigrant Middle Class in Bayonne, New Jersey, 1915–1925," *Labor History* 25 (Winter 1984): 51–82

Charles W. Churchill, *The Italians of Newark: A Community Study* (New York, 1975)

John T. Cunningham, *Newark*

John A. DeBrizzi, "The Standard Oil Strikes in Bayonne, New Jersey, 1915–1916," *New Jersey History* 101 (Fall/Winter 1983): 1–11

Michael Ebner, "Strikes and Society: Civil Behavior in Passaic, 1875–1926," *New Jersey History* 97 (Spring 1979): 7–24

John Higham, *Strangers in the Land: Patterns of American Nativism, 1860–1925* (New Brunswick, 1955)

Irving Howe, *World of Our Fathers* (New York, 1976)

Junior Order United American Mechanics, *Official Minutes of the State Council* (Trenton, 1915) and "Official Program ... Commemorating the 47th Annual Convention of the New Jersey State Council," (Newark, 1915)

Israel Kasovich, *The Days of Our Years* (New York, 1929)

Timothy J. Meager, "Irish All the Time: Ethnic Consciousness Among the Irish in Worcester, Massachusetts, 1880–1905," *Journal of Social History* 19 (Winter 1985): 273–304

"The Patriotic Order Sons of America: Something About the Order," (Philadelphia, 1888)

Sackett, *Modern Battles of Trenton*, vol. 1

Morris Schonbach, *Radicals and Visionaries: A History of Dissent in New Jersey* (Princeton, 1964)

Philip A. M. Taylor, *The Distant Magnet: European Emigration to the U.S.A.* (New York, 1971)

Vecoli, *People of New Jersey*

And: Federal Manuscript Census Schedules of Jersey City, New Jersey, 1860, Roll 653–693.

Chapter Four

E. Digby Baltzell, *The Protestant Establishment: Aristocracy & Caste in America* (New York, 1964): Bodnar, *The Transplanted*

Martha E. Bruere, *Does Prohibition Work?* (New York, 1927)

Bukowcyzk, "The Transformation of Working Class Ethnicity"

Joseph W. Carlevale, *Americans of Italian Descent in New Jersey* (Clifton, 1950)

David M. Chalmers, *Hooded Americanism* (New York, 1968)

Church of St. Casimir, *Dedication* (n.p., 1962)

Churchill *The Italians of Newark*

Richard J. Connors, *A Cycle of Power: The Career of Jersey City Mayor Frank Hague* (Metuchen, 1971)

Barbara Cunningham, ed., *The New Jersey Ethnic Experience* (Union City, 1977)

Leonard Dinnerstein and David Reimers, *Ethnic Americans: A History of Immigration and Assimilation* (New York, 1975)

Higham, *Strangers in the Land* and *Send These to Me: Jews and Other Immigrants in Urban America* (New York, 1975)

Kenneth Jackson, *The Ku Klux Klan in the City, 1915–1930* (New York, 1967)

Charles H. Mindel and Robert W. Habenstein, eds., *Ethnic Families in America: Patterns and Variations* (New York, 1981)

Michael Novak, *The Rise of the Unmeltable Ethnics* (New York, 1972)

Oral history interview with Ernest D. Shaw, December 1986, Dade City, Florida and diary of Vincent C. Shaw, March–December 1906, copy in author's possession

Vecoli, *People of New Jersey*

Morris R. Werb, "Jewish Suburbia—An Historical and Comparative Study of Jewish Communities in Three New Jersey Suburbs" (Ph.D. diss., New York University, 1959).

Chapter Five

Pastora San Juan Cafferty, et. al., *The Dilemma of American Immigration: Beyond the Golden Door* (New Brunswick, 1983)

John Crewdson, *The Tarnished Door: The New Immigrants and the Transformation of America* (New York, 1983)

Barbara Cunningham, *The New Jersey Ethnic Experience*

Dinnerstein and Reimers, *Ethnic Americans*

Vivian Garrison and Carol I. Weiss, "Dominican Family Networks and United States Immigration Policy: A Case Study," *IMR: International Migration Review* 13 (Summer 1979): 264–83

Nathan Glazer and Daniel P. Moynihan, *Beyond the Melting Pot: The Negroes, Puerto Ricans, Jews, Italians and Irish of New York City,* 2nd. ed. (Cambridge, Mass., 1970)

Marie Gonzales, "Focusing on Puerto Ricans—Hispanics in Newark," in *From Riot to Recovery: Newark After Ten Years,* ed. Stanley B. Winters (Washington, D.C., 1979): 97–104

Illsoo Kim, *New Urban Immigrants: The Korean Community in New York* (Princeton, 1981)

1984 Statistical Yearbook of the Immigration and Naturalization Service (Washington, D.C., 1984)

Leo Pap, *The Portuguese Americans* (Boston, 1981)

David M. Reimers, *Still the Golden Door: The Third World Comes to America* (New York, 1985)

Eleanor Meyer Rogg, *The Assimilation of Cuban Exiles: The Role of Community and Class* (New York, 1974)

Lawrence Wissbeski, "The Police—Puerto Rican Riots: Newark, 1974," in *From Riot to Recovery,* 105–15

U.S. Bureau of the Census, Summary Population and Housing Characteristics, 1990 (Washington, D.C., 1991)

And these newspapers and magazines: *The New York Times,* 5 June 1958, 16 July 1959, 3 June 1960, 17 February 1975, 5 June 1986, *Time,* 8 July 1985, *The Wall Street Journal,* 8 October 1984, 29 January 1987, *The Washington Post,* 7 July 1980.

Conclusion

Nathan Glazer, "Bilingualism: Will It Work?" in Glazer, *Ethnic Dilemmas,* 1964–1982 (Cambridge, Mass., 1983): 135–56
Thomas Muller, "Economic Effects of Immigration," in *Glamor at the Gates: The New American Immigration,* ed. Nathan Glazer (San Francisco, Calif., 1985): 109–33
Reimers, *Still the Golden Door*
And these newspapers and magazines: *Time,* 8 July 1985, *The Wall Street Journal,* 28 November 1986, *The Washington Post,* 7 July 1980.

SUGGESTIONS FOR FURTHER READING

Full bibliographic citations are given in this section only for titles not listed elsewhere. All other titles are fully cited in *Sources*, p. 78.

The most complete work on immigrants and ethnicity in New Jersey remains Rudolph J. Vecoli's *The People of New Jersey* (Princeton, 1965). As it contains an extensive bibliography of works published before 1963, this essay will concentrate on works appearing subsequently.

Two general works deserve mention. Philip A. M. Taylor's *The Distant Magnet: European Emigration to the U.S.A.* (New York, 1971) covers the process of immigration down to the 1920s. John Bodnar's *The Transplanted: A History of Immigrants in Urban America* (Bloomington, Ind., 1985) examines immigrant communities and their adaptation to industrial cities.

There is interesting first-person material in the seven completed numbers of the New Jersey Historical Commission's New Jersey Ethnic Life Series, edited by Howard L. Green (Trenton, 1986–1987). The series is based on oral history interviews conducted in the late 1970s. Another source of interview material is *America, the Dream of My Life: Selections from the Federal Writers' Project's New Jersey Ethnic Survey,* edited by David Steven Cohen (New Brunswick, 1990).

The colonial and early national periods in New Jersey are covered in John E. Pomfret, *Colonial New Jersey: A History* (New York, 1973), and Richard P. McCormick, *New Jersey from Colony to State,* rev. ed., (Newark, 1981). More specialized are Adrian C. Leiby, *The Early Dutch and Swedish Settlers of New Jersey* (New York, 1964), and Wesley Frank Craven, *New Jersey and the English Colonization of North America* (New York, 1964). The size and nature of colonial ethnic groups is explored by Thomas L. Purvis in "The European Origins of New Jersey's

Eighteenth Century Population," *New Jersey History,* Spring/
Summer 1982.

New Jersey's nineteenth-century immigrants are less satisfac-
torily served. Raymond M. Ralph, in "The City and the Church:
Catholic Beginnings in Newark, 1840–1870," *New Jersey History,*
Autumn/Winter 1978, shows the relationship between the
church and Newark's Irish. John Cunningham includes brief
sketches of many ethnic groups in *Newark* (Newark, 1966).
Douglas V. Shaw, in *The Making of an Immigrant City: Ethnic
and Cultural Conflict in Jersey City, 1850–1877* (New York, 1976),
covers the Irish and Germans and their conflicts with the native-
born. Several essays in Herbert G. Gutman's *Work, Culture and
Society in Industrializing America: Essays in American Working-
Class and Social History* (New York, 1976) deal with immigrants
in Paterson.

Charles W. Churchill's *The Italians of Newark: A Community
Study* (New York, 1975) takes that group from 1880 through
the Great Depression. Information on Poles in Hudson County
can be found in John A. DeBrizzi, "The Standard Oil Strikes
in Bayonne, New Jersey, 1915–1916," *New Jersey History,* Fall/
Winter 1983, and John J. Bukowczyk, "The Transformation of
Working Class Ethnicity: Corporate Control, Americanization,
and the Polish Immigrant Middle Class In Bayonne, New Jersey,
1915–1925," *Labor History,* Winter 1984. Aspects of the Jewish
experience are noted in Joseph Brandes, *Immigrants to Freedom:
Jewish Communities in Rural New Jersey Since 1882*
(Philadelphia, 1971), and Morris R. Werb, *Jewish Suburbia—
An Historical and Comparative Study of Jewish Communities in
Three New Jersey Suburbs* (Ph.D. dissertation, New York Univer-
sity, 1959).

The essays edited by Barbara Cunningham in *The New Jersey
Ethnic Experience* (Union City, 1977) treat thirty-one different
ethnic groups, many of them fairly small. They represent
primarily the "old" and "new" immigrant nationalities.

Third-world immigration is well covered in David Reimers,
Still the Golden Door: The Third World Comes to America (New
York, 1985); it has an extensive bibliography. Eleanor M. Rogg's
*The Assimilation of Cuban Exiles: The Role of Community and
Class* (New York, 1974) studies Hispanics in West New York.
The themes in Illsoo Kim's excellent *New Urban Immigrants:
The Korean Community in New York* (Princeton, 1981) apply

also to New Jersey. Other recent immigrant groups to New Jersey still await study.